Film: The Essential Study Guide

Providing a key resource to new students, *Film: The Essential Study Guide* introduces students to all the skills they will need to learn to succeed on a film studies course.

This succinct, accessible guide covers key topics such as:

- using the library
- online research and resources
- viewing skills
- how to watch and study foreign language films
- essay writing
- presentation skills
- referencing and plagiarism
- practical filmmaking.

Including exercises and examples, *Film: The Essential Study Guide* helps film students understand how study skills are applicable to their learning and gives them the tools to flourish in their degree.

Ruth Doughty is a Senior Lecturer in Film Studies at Portsmouth University. Her specific areas of research are Black American cinema, film music and films that explore national guilt in a post-9/11 context. She has recently co-edited *The Continuum Companion to Sound and Film in the Visual Media*. She has published articles on Kassovitz's *La Haine* and von Trier's *Manderlay*. At present she is co-authoring a book on Film Theory for Palgrave Macmillan.

Deborah Shaw is a Reader in Film Studies at Portsmouth University. Her research area is Latin American Cinema, and she has published numerous articles in this field. She has also published *Contemporary Latin American Cinema: Ten Key Films* (Continuum, 2003) and is the editor of *Contemporary Latin American Cinema: Breaking into the Global Market* (Rowman and Littlefield, 2007).

Film: The Essential Study Guide

Edited by
Ruth Doughty and
Deborah Shaw

 Routledge
Taylor & Francis Group

LONDON AND NEW YORK

2/17/09
ww
#24.95

First published 2009
by Routledge
2 Park Square, Milton Park, Abingdon, Oxon OX14 4RN

Simultaneously published in the USA and Canada
by Routledge
270 Madison Ave, New York, NY 10016

Routledge is an imprint of the Taylor & Francis Group, an informa business

© 2009 Ruth Doughty and Deborah Shaw for editorial matter and
selection; individual chapters, the contributors

Typeset in Perpetua and Bell Gothic by
Book Now Ltd, London
Printed and bound in Great Britain by
CPI Antony Rowe, Chippenham, Wiltshire

British Library Cataloguing in Publication Data
A catalogue record for this book is available from the British Library

Library of Congress Cataloging in Publication Data
A catalog record has been requested

ISBN10: 0–415–43700–8 (pbk)
ISBN10: 0–203–00292–X (ebk)

ISBN13: 978–0–415–43700–4 (pbk)
ISBN13: 978–0–203–00292–6 (ebk)

To the Film Studies students at
Portsmouth University:
past, present and future

Contents

List of figures

Contributors

DAVE ALLEN is Head of the School of Creative Arts Film and Media at Portsmouth University. He began his academic life as a teacher of art and design but for the past 25 years has also been involved in teaching film and media studies. For many years his principal research focus has been on visual arts pedagogy. In recent years he has published in the field of British cultural practices, including film, media and popular music.

CRAIG BATTY is Senior Lecturer in Media Writing at the University of Portsmouth. His research and practical expertise are in the area of screenwriting, and he freelances as a script and story consultant. He has published many articles on the practice and theory of screenwriting, and is co-author of the book *Writing for the Screen: Creative and Critical Approaches* (Palgrave Macmillan, 2008). He is currently co-writing *Media Writing* (Palgrave Macmillan, forthcoming).

LOUISE BUCKLER and SIMON HOBBS are third-year Film Studies students at the University of Portsmouth. After their degrees both are planning to continue in Portsmouth to undertake a Masters in Film and Television.

RÉKA BUCKLEY is Senior Lecturer in Film Studies at Portsmouth University. She completed her PhD in 2002 on 'The Female

Film Star in Post-war Italy (1948–60)' at Royal Holloway, University of London. Her research interests include stars and their consumption by audiences, stars in Italian cinema and fashion, national identity and fandom. She has published several articles on the post-war Italian star system, and on fashion in film. She is currently completing a book on the Italian post-war star system.

RUTH DOUGHTY is a Senior Lecturer in Film Studies at Portsmouth University. Her specific areas of research are Black American cinema, film music and films that explore national guilt in a post-9/11 context. She has recently co-edited *The Continuum Companion to Sound and Film in the Visual Media*. She has published articles on Kassovitz's *La Haine* and von Trier's *Manderlay*. At present she is co-authoring a book on Film Theory for Palgrave Macmillan.

EMMA DYSON is a Lecturer in Film Studies and Media Studies at the University of Portsmouth. She teaches at all levels of the Film Studies degree in Portsmouth. She is also currently studying and writing for her PhD on aspects of the Cinematic Zombie.

LAURIE EDE is a Principal Lecturer in Film and Television at the University of Portsmouth. He has produced articles on many different aspects of British screen culture and he takes a particular interest in film aesthetics. Laurie is currently writing a comprehensive history of British film production design. *British film design: a history* will be published by I.B.Tauris.

CHRISTINE ETHERINGTON-WRIGHT teaches film and literature at undergraduate and post-graduate level at the University of Portsmouth. Her book *Gender, Professions and Discourse: early twentieth century women's autobiography* is due to be published in November 2008. Christine's current research is on the discourse of women in British films and literary adaptations of the 1950s to 1990s.

LAUREL FORSTER is a Senior Lecturer in print media and television studies at the University of Portsmouth. Her research interests are in women's writing, women's culture and representations of the domestic in various media forms and genres. Her publications are on a range of subjects including women's writing of the modernist period, feminist magazines, domestic television programmes, and science fiction films and television series. She is currently working on a longer study of women's magazines.

DAVID FRANCIS was for many years Humanities Librarian at the University of Portsmouth. Teaching library skills to Film Studies students at all levels was an important part of his job.

GRETA FRIGGENS is Faculty Librarian for Creative and Cultural Industries at the University of Portsmouth. Working closely with the School of Creative Arts, Film and Media she is responsible for developing collections to support learning, teaching and research. One of her main priorities is developing and delivering information literacy programmes to enable students to efficiently utilise the growing wealth of information.

LINCOLN GERAGHTY is Principal Lecturer in Film Studies and Subject Leader for Media Studies in the School of Creative Arts, Film and Media at the University of Portsmouth. He serves as editorial advisor for *The Journal of Popular Culture*, *Reconstruction* and *Atlantis*, with interests in science-fiction film and television, fandom and collecting in popular culture. He is author of *Living with Star Trek: American Culture and the Star Trek Universe* (I.B.Tauris, 2007) and *American Science Fiction Film and Television* (Berg, forthcoming) and the editor of *The Influence of Star Trek on Television, Film and Culture* (McFarland, 2008), with Mark Jancovich *The Shifting Definitions of Genre: Essays on Labeling Film, Television Shows and Media* (McFarland, 2008), and *Future Visions: Examining the Look of Science Fiction and Fantasy Television* (Scarecrow, forthcoming).

xiii

SUE HARPER is Professor of Film History at Portsmouth University. She has written widely on British cinema, and teaches on every level of the Film Studies degree at Portsmouth. She has written many articles on British cinema, and her books include: *Picturing the Past: the Rise and Fall of the British Costume Film* (British Film Institute, 1994), *Women in British Cinema: Mad, Bad and Dangerous to Know* (Continuum, 2000), *British Cinema of the 1950s: the Decline of Deference* (Oxford University Press, 2007), with Vincent Porter, and *The New Film History*, co-edited with James Chapman and Mark Glancy (Palgrave MacMillan, 2007). Sue is the Principle Investigator of the major AHRC project at Portsmouth on 1970s British cinema.

VAN NORRIS is a Film and Media Studies Lecturer at the University of Portsmouth. His teaching and research interests lie within the study of American graphic narratives, popular and alternative forms of American and European animation and aspects of British and American television and film comedy. Among his published works are: 'Interior Logic: Appropriations of Surrealism into Popular American Animation', in *The Unsilvered Screen: Surrealism and Cinema*, G. Harper and R. Stone, 2007, 'John Barry – 007 and Counting', in *The Continuum Companion to Sound in Film and the Visual Media*, G. Harper (ed.), 2008, and 'Yeah looks like it n'all . . . ' – Mapping the relationship between the 'live action' universe, abridged figurative design and computer animation within 'Modern Toss' in *Animation – An Interdisciplinary Journal*, 2008.

DYLAN PANK is a Tutor in video production skills. For the past 13 years he has collaborated on short films, independent documentaries and experimental and animated films, as a writer, director, sound recordist, sound designer, editor and visual effects supervisor. His work has been seen (and heard) in film festivals and on TV broadcasts around the world. He has taught video production, editing and sound for film for five years at Istanbul Bilgi University, and currently teaches video production skills at the University of Portsmouth.

KAREN SAVAGE is Senior Lecturer in Creative and Performing Arts at the University of Portsmouth. She has exhibited film and video work in a number of international festivals, and she is Director of the *Sixty Second Film and Video Festival*. Continuously working with practitioners and academics she explores the thresholds between practice and theory, and she has recently published Black to White: The Fading Process of Intermediality in the *Journal of Culture, Language and Representation* May 2008. She is a member of the Intermediality Working Group as part of the International Federation for Theatre Research; she is currently co-editing the working group's second publication.

DEBORAH SHAW is a Reader in Film Studies at Portsmouth University. Her research area is Latin American Cinema, and she has published numerous articles in this field. She has also published *Contemporary Latin American Cinema: Ten Key Films* (Continuum, 2003) and is the editor of *Contemporary Latin American Cinema: Breaking into the Global Market* (Rowman and Littlefield, 2007).

JUSTIN SMITH is Principal Lecturer and Subject Leader for Film Studies at the University of Portsmouth, UK. A cultural historian with a specialism in British cinema, his research interests and writing cover film fandom, reception and exhibition cultures and issues of identity and memory. He has published articles in *The Journal of British Cinema and Television* and *Fashion Theory* and has recently contributed a chapter on web ethnography to *The New Film History* (Palgrave/Macmillan, 2007). He is currently writing a book entitled *Cult Films and Film Cults in British Cinema, 1968–86*.

PAUL SPICER is a PhD student and lecturer at the University of Portsmouth with an expertise in East Asian and especially Japanese cinema history. He is currently writing his thesis on film director Kenji Mizoguchi. Paul is responsible for the Japanese Cinema and Culture and East Asian Film Studies units.

Chapter 1

Studying film at university

Sue Harper

Why study film at university? On the face of it, this looks like a simple question which could elicit simple answers – 'because I enjoyed studying film at 6th form college', 'because it will help me towards a career as a film director'. Answers like these, though, won't get us very far. Film Studies, like other academic disciplines, needs its students to be driven by a passion for the subject in all its forms, and Film Studies students need to have an intellectual hunger for knowledge about all aspects of the moving image. This desire to understand the inner workings of the cinema should be the first qualification for a student of film.

It would be mistaken to expect a degree in Film Studies to provide an instant gateway to work as a film director or producer, even though some courses contain practical film production units. Attention to the careers of many directors and producers such as Quentin Tarantino, Nicolas Roeg or David Puttnam will find little evidence of formal academic training in their field, though of course their work displays knowledge of film movements. Rather, major figures in the film industry tend to arrive at the pinnacle of their craft by hard training, by guile, instinct, good luck or just plain accident: being in the right place at the right time.

The reason we should study film at university is because the cinema is the art form which is most urgently linked with mass taste, and with an artistic creativity intimately linked to technology. The academic study of it, therefore, will help us to do three things:

1

to understand the taste of audiences, to understand the roots and workings of creativity in an industrial and technological context, and to help us to think through the way in which film culture responds critically to social and political issues. To do this properly, the Film Studies student needs to look rigorously at different forms of evidence, and to weigh and measure various theoretical approaches. But above all, he or she needs to recognise the crucial role of *pleasure* in the analysis of cinema. There is an intimate relationship between audience pleasure and producers' profits; audiences will only flock to see films which help them to interpret the world in a pleasurable way. Mainstream films can please their audiences in a relatively straightforward way, while experimental films, which appeal to niche markets and are shown in art cinemas, can give pleasure by stimulating or even puzzling their audiences. The cinema can provide us with vital evidence about ways of seeing. The Film Studies student should also be able to locate the sources of the creative pleasures of the film's makers: who did what and why, and how much creative autonomy did they have during the process of production?

So we can see that, if it is to be comprehensive and academically respectable, the study of film cannot just be text-based. It should not just be a list of favourites, or a recital of the story-line of key films. The study of film should look at the surface of the film itself, of course – its visual style, its composition – but it must also look at its historical and industrial context, in order to find out what it meant for the society that produced it. And that holds good for films made in 2008 as well as for those produced in 1934.

Without doubt, film is the most powerful medium society has for influencing mass audiences: hence the 'moral panics' orchestrated by establishment figures and gatekeepers of public opinion in the early days of the cinema. It was thought by many figures in positions of social authority that cinema wielded a dangerous power. This panic was exacerbated by the coming of sound, since that led to an increase in mass audiences and to official fears that they were being fed pap which would have a serious effect on their sexual morality or political views. So cultural commentators realised right from the outset that cinema performed a vital role in society, because it has a powerful effect on the consciousness of the viewer.

It is part of the film student's remit to account for the extraordinary power of the image over audiences. He or she should try to produce a well-informed analysis of the reasons why certain film stars or certain genres flowered in some periods and not in others – why the Western genre was so prolific in Hollywood in the 1940s and 1950s, or why audiences empathised with (say) Marilyn Monroe and not with a more minor star from the same period. To be sure, some of the Film Studies student's analysis of such issues will be based on speculation: but most of it ought to rely on a familiarity with the production system of the period, on a knowledge of mundane things like profits-and-losses, and on a solid understanding of the way in which people felt in the past, and the way artists dealt with technology.

It is commonly argued that what cinema does is to offer an 'escape' from the real world. The problem with such an argument is that it is too general. What the film student should do is to recognise the complexity of tasks which the cinema can fulfil. To be sure, it can just provide an escape from the everyday. The 1930s musicals of Fred Astaire and Ginger Rogers can be interpreted like this, though on closer examination they also provide a lot of information about notions of taste, dress and patterns of consumption. But more importantly, cinema can provide powerful metaphors for audiences which will help them to address important anxieties in their lives and to redress them. Thus melodramas can help female audiences to think through issues about their own families and feelings, while 'action' films can encourage male viewers to think about masculinity, power and responsibility. A little further down the line, of course, we could think about the role of the male viewer of melodrama, or the development of the female action movie. Speculating about the social function of a film is one of the most exciting aspects

3

of film study, though a student's work should be based on some evidence about the way a film was received or interpreted.

Besides looking at the social meaning of cinema, what else ought a Film Studies student to do? He or she will need to realise that cinema is a *process*. I suggested earlier that, although Film Studies as a discipline originally focused on the text itself, it has latterly been thought necessary to work on the production context too. A film goes through four processes: *production*: *distribution*: *exhibition*: *reception*. Let us look at each of these in turn, and consider what the Film Studies student needs to do with them.

When we look at a film's *production*, it is important to recognise that the final film is the result of a complex series of negotiations. A finished film can be seen as the result of struggles which took place before and during its production. A student needs to try to find out whose creativity was dominant – the producer's, the scriptwriter's, the designer's or the director's. Another way of putting this is to say that the student needs to assess the *agency* and *autonomy* of different workers on the film. Often it is handy to use interview material here, but this always needs to be done with care, since most interviewees want to place themselves in the best possible light. We might also consider whether or not processes which took place after filming, such as editing, music or marketing, materially altered the meaning of the text.

For a proper study of the way films are consumed in society, *distribution* is important. What this means is that we need to know about cinema circuits and their power, and to recognise that distributors are the ones who decide which films are shown, and for how long. Sometimes films are not popular simply because distributors have decided (for example) only to show them in unimportant cinemas, or indeed to release them straight onto video. *Exhibition* is an important aspect of cinema too, and the study of cinemas themselves, their location, their architecture and their status can be an important way of looking at the consumption process. Often students can undertake local studies into these areas via research compiled from local newspapers, and they can thus do primary research into the role of the cinema in local communities.

The reception of films is a more thorny issue. There are two sorts of reception studies: critical reception, or audience reception. If a student wants to show how a film was received by critics, it is important to give a sense of balanced coverage. It is no good just quoting a positive review from the film critic of *The Times* and then lamely concluding that a film was generally well received. If possible, something from trade papers and something from the lower-status dailies would need to be included as well. When it comes to audience response, one has to cut one's coat according to one's cloth. Often surveys are unbalanced in terms of gender, age and class, and we have to take this into account. Sometimes there is simply no material at all about what audiences actually thought about a film, or if there is, then it is filtered through powerful gate-keepers who usually have an axe to grind. In our own period, we are fortunate in having access to the internet, and fan-based sites can provide valuable evidence about the way people perceive films as influencing them. But we need to use these with care.

The Film Studies student also needs to have an acute sense of visual style. This is not a sort of excrescence laid on top of the 'real' text of words and narrative. Rather, a film's visual texture – its lighting, composition, art direction and costume design – help us to see where it stands in relation to other artistic practices of its period, such as painting. But in this area, the Film Studies student has to be able to use analyses which are historically informed. He or she needs to know when (say) Eastmancolor came in, or the advantages or disadvantages of Technicolor or the innovations permitted by the Arriflex camera. Then proper judgements can be made about the 'look' of a film.

Of course, Film Studies varies a lot from one educational institution to another. Courses have been devised and are staffed by academics who come from a range of backgrounds including Modern Languages, History, English Literature and American

5

Studies. Younger members of staff are more likely to have come from the disciplines of Film or Media Studies. Some degree courses have a very strong bias towards theory; others have much less. But what unites all degrees in this field is that their teachers and students share a belief in the cultural, social and artistic significance of their medium. The discipline of Film Studies seeks to explain film's importance, and to evaluate the creativities involved in it. In a sense, the Film Studies student aims to be a cultural historian as well as a film buff and, in their academic work, he or she goes out to meet – in spirit at least – the people who made and enjoyed the films they study.

Chapter 2

The independent student

Ruth Doughty and Deborah Shaw

PREPARATION FOR DISCUSSION

Quickly jot down 10 things that characterise the good student and 10 characteristics that are typically associated with the poor student.

INTRODUCTION

At university you are largely left to your own devices. You will be issued with a timetable, given assignments and deadlines and then expected to get on with it. This can be both liberating and daunting for students used to following a more prescribed schedule. In this chapter we will give you tips on how to balance your time between academic study and relaxation, whilst also providing pointers on how to get the most from your degree. We will also consider how you can benefit from the support systems that are in place at all institutions in case you are feeling overwhelmed or are experiencing any problems.

PREPARATION FOR CLASS

It is important to be prepared for both lectures and seminars. Here are some tips and suggestions:

- Before the class do some reading around the subject focusing on such areas as: the director, the film movement, genre and national context.
- Ask your lecturer for advice regarding additional films related to the topic and watch some of these films in your own time.
- Search the internet for relevant material relating to what you are about to study.
- Look at the reading list for the unit and identify texts that will complement what you learn in class; then go to the library to track down these books.

TIME MANAGEMENT AND ORGANISATION

When you arrive at university one of the first things you will notice is that you will be treated as an adult. However, this brings with it certain expectations and responsibilities. As a Film Studies student you will not have contact with the academic staff from 9–5 Monday to Friday. Instead you will have around 10 hours of contact time, more if you include practical film-making and screenings. Therefore, it is important that you use your time wisely and know what is expected of you.

The following table includes some examples of how you can best manage non-contact time while at home and at university.

At Home	At University
Keep on top of any material that you can access through your university's virtual learning environment.	If you have a couple of hours between lectures, go to the library and locate some key texts for your assignment.

At Home	At University
If you have a seminar at midday, watch a film relevant to your unit.	During a free period go to your resource centre/library and take out a film that will be relevant to your studies.
Write up your lecture notes, and organise handouts etc.	Find quiet places where you can work in peace in between lectures. It is surprising how much you can do in a short space of time.

PRODUCING A PERSONAL TIMETABLE

A glance at a typical academic timetable (shaded area on the version 1 timetable) gives you the impression that you have a lot of free time; however, this is misleading. Below there are two versions of Quentin Scorsese's first-year timetable. Version 1 is that given to him by the university, version 2 is the timetable that he has personalised to use his non-classroom time in an efficient and responsible manner.

We haven't included evenings as this is up to you, but this is an ideal time to catch up on any films that may have been referenced in lectures, or any reading that is required, or essay/exam preparation. If you are up to date with your studies then why not read the most recent reviews in either the broadsheet newspapers or specialist film journals such as *Sight and Sound*. Alternatively, have a look at what's on at your local commercial or art house cinema.

Quentin Scorsese's timetable: year 1, version 1

	Monday	Tuesday	Wednesday	Thursday	Friday
09.00	Film Theory Lecture				Cinema and Nation Seminar
10.00			Cinema and Nation Lecture		Film Language Screening
11.00	Film Language Lecture				Film Language Screening
12.00		Video Production Lecture	Film Language Seminar		
13.00	Cinema and Nation Screening				
14.00	Cinema and Nation Screening				
15.00		Film Theory Seminar	Video Production Seminar		
16.00					
17.00					

Quentin Scorsese's timetable: year 1, version 2

	Monday	Tuesday	Wednesday	Thursday	Friday
09.00	Film Theory Lecture	ZZZ	ZZZ	ZZZ	Cinema and Nation Seminar
10.00	Library/ Resources	Watch Film	Cinema and Nation Lecture	Private Study	Film Language Screening
11.00	Film Language Lecture	Watch Film	Library/ Resources	Private Study	Film Language Screening
12.00	Lunch + Private Study	Video Production Lecture	Film Language Seminar	Private Study	Library/ Resources
13.00	Cinema and Nation Screening	Lunch	Lunch	Lunch	Lunch
14.00	Cinema and Nation Screening	Private Study	Private Study	Private Study	Private Study
15.00	Gym	Film Theory Seminar	Video Production Seminar	Watch Film	Private Study
16.00	Private Study	Private Study	Swim	Watch Film	Pub
17.00	Leisure time	Leisure time	Leisure time	Leisure time	Pub

SEMINAR EXERCISE

Produce a personalised timetable based on the above model. Remember to make it realistic and to find a good balance between academic study, relaxation and socialising with friends.

GETTING INVOLVED

Film Studies is a degree programme that is usually chosen because students have a passion for the subject. There are many things that you can do to take your interest in film beyond the classroom. Here are a few ideas:

- Start a Film Society.
- Help organise a university Film Festival.
- Volunteer as the course representative for Staff/Student Committees.
- Organise trips to cinemas/Film Festivals/museums.
- Provide staff with constructive feedback on the course.
- Find out about film-making competitions and help organise a submission from your course.
- Get involved with any student union activities relating to film.

PASTORAL CARE

There is plenty of support for students at universities from a range of people including your friends, lecturers, counsellors and wardens or resident tutors within university accommodation. However, they will not come looking for you in times of trouble, you need to seek them out. It is strongly recommended that you inform your personal tutor or appropriate lecturer of any issues that are affecting your work so that they can help you in a variety of ways.

Lecturers are rarely shocked at students' problems, and their job is to support you, not judge you. It is important to find a member of staff whom you feel comfortable talking to. The chances are that lecturers will have experienced other students facing similar problems and what you say can remain confidential. At times, other staff will need to know that there have been problems so that they understand absences or failure to submit work, but they do not need to know any details.

Living in halls and student flats can also be a major source of conflict. Noise levels, personal relationships and who bought the last roll of toilet paper or loaf of bread can lead to upsetting disputes. All universities have support networks in place and wardens or resident tutors can help to mediate and resolve issues. Alternatively, if you are living in a private house with fellow students and problems occur, you can go and talk to staff at the student support centre.

All universities offer a free counselling service where you have an opportunity to discuss any problems that you may be experiencing. All matters will be treated confidentially and counsellors will not divulge any information to academic staff or indeed anyone, but they can write a letter of support for you on request.

Students, like anyone else, can experience a range of personal issues that can make coping with university life very difficult.

Some potential problems include:

- Physical and mental illness
- Self-harming
- Eating disorders
- Drug and alcohol dependency
- Unwanted pregnancy
- Financial problems
- Agoraphobia
- Panic attacks
- Fear of public speaking, giving presentations

- Family problems
- Relationship problems
- Sexual abuse
- Bereavement
- Cultural or religious differences
- Isolation
- Difficulty adapting to university life

Remember that you are not alone, and even though you are away from home, the university and its staff are there to support you. Don't suffer in silence, as there are support networks in place to help you when you are facing difficulties. Most universities have a system whereby extenuating circumstances are taken into account if your academic work suffers. Make sure that you are aware of the procedures, and take advantage of the help available to you.

Chapter 3

University life: the student perspective

Louise Buckler and Simon Hobbs

INTRODUCTION

The transition to university life can be a daunting prospect for new students. The university way of life requires many changes that you may not have had to deal with before, such as moving away from home, budgeting, living with strangers and learning independently. This chapter, written by students, will explore both the academic and social sides of university life. It will try to provide you with helpful tips and advice to help you cope with some of the problems you may face whilst at university.

THE TRANSITION TO UNIVERSITY

The move to university can be a big transition for many students. The learning process differs in many ways to what you may be used to. In most universities you will attend lectures with a large number of other students instead of being taught in small classes. Usually the lectures you attend will include most of the students on the film course, which can initially be a daunting prospect. Within lectures, you are not required to interact as you would in a seminar or tutorial as the main emphasis is on taking notes and listening to the lecturer.

The biggest transition when arriving at university concerns the style of learning. Here a much more independent style of learning is

15

required; you will not be in lectures, viewings and seminars all day, every day. You will have many gaps and lots of free time during which you are expected to do your own work such as reading recommended texts from reading lists provided, researching, writing essays and viewing films relating to your study. University gives you much more freedom; you are not told repeatedly that hand-in dates are near or that you should have started your work. This is left in your hands so organisation is an essential tool.

DYSLEXIC STUDENTS

The transition to university can be particularly intimidating for students who experience any form of learning difficulties, the most common of which is dyslexia. This section written by a student with dyslexia discusses some of the problems students may experience and provides some tips to manage the condition at university.

Having dyslexia can make education a daunting prospect. However, universities have many ways to aid your learning, such as providing students with extra time during exams and giving you an allowance for photocopying, printing and academic texts. Universities also employ learning support staff; they offer support on aspects such as essay writing and structure and provide you with help and advice concerning other academic areas. They will also give you information about how to apply for extra funding for equipment and textbooks. It can also be a good idea to talk to your tutor and lecturers and explain your situation so they can offer you the support you need.

SOME PROBLEMS AND ADVICE

■ Structuring essays can be a problem; try to choose questions that have a structure built in, such as, 'Assess the birth and death of Italian Neorealism'.

- If you are still unsure about your structure arrange to see your lecturer and see if they can provide any tips. You can also ask your friends how they structure their essays.
- Spelling can be less of an issue at university than at school or college, as most work (excluding exams) is word-processed.
- It is a good idea to learn the spelling of certain film terms, as well as directors and movements.
- Many lecturers use PowerPoint, which will help with the spelling of key words.
- Reading can be hard work, and at university you are required to read a lot. The most important thing here is to give yourself time to read the work.
- Accept any help that is available, including extra time and the book allowance.

Many of these points are not exclusive to students suffering from learning difficulties as they can be helpful for everyone.

Although you may, at times, find university hard, what you have to remember is that you will not be the only one who has dyslexia and that institutions are fully equipped to offer help and support if and when you need it.

HALLS

Living in halls of residence will differ greatly from the accommodation that many of you will be accustomed to. Many university halls consist of communal living spaces, so although you may have a private bedroom, you will share your living room and kitchen with other students. For many students, coming to university means moving away from home for the first time. This can result in many emotions, including fear and relief. It can be a very worrying time, yet it is important to know that you are not alone, and many other students will be feeling the same as you.

17

Advantages and disadvantages of living in Halls:

Advantages

Halls are linked directly to the university so any problems such as broken or faulty facilities and lost keys can be quickly resolved.

Moving into halls allows you to be surrounded by other students, so halls are a great way to get to know people who are not on your course.

Halls provide a great safety net, because while you will not be living with your parents you are still supported by the university.

Disadvantages

The balance between work and play can be a hard one to strike when living in halls. Your friends on different courses may have different deadlines from you, meaning you may be working while they are free.

As you will be living in a new environment with new people, tensions between housemates can arise.

Noise can be a common complaint when living in halls of residence and can result in many sleepless nights and disrupt your studies.

If any problems do arise try and talk to one another about the issues; if this does not work, consider seeking the advice of a resident tutor or hall warden. These are typically post-graduate students connected to the student support network. Another option is talking to your tutor, who may be able to offer you advice and help, particularly if your work is suffering.

NIGHTS OUT

The social side of university can be quite a big factor for many students. The fact that many of you will be living away from home amongst a large student community will mean that socialising will consume a lot of your time, especially within the first few weeks. As many of you will be moving to a completely different area, the best thing to do is to try and find out what the town has to offer.

Friendly Advice for Freshers:

- Try and stick to the more student-friendly pubs and areas in the city.
- Some clubs and pubs may have student nights at which drinks can be cheaper, as can entry. This means that you can have cheaper nights out, as well as having fun with people in the same situation as you.
- A heavy night out will often result in a hangover. This can have a serious effect the next day, so if you have a deadline or lectures all day try to drink responsibly.

What you will have to remember, however, is that going out doesn't have to be specifically aimed at the pub and club environments; make sure that you find out what else your city has to offer such as cinemas, bowling alleys and sport facilities to provide you with a variety of choices depending on your mood.

CLUBS AND SOCIETIES

Clubs and societies are a great way of socialising. The diversity of clubs and societies means that it is almost guaranteed that there will be at least one that you will have an interest in. Here you will have the chance to meet like-minded people.

Before joining any clubs or societies do make sure that you are aware of the costs involved as some of the more active clubs (such as snowboarding and paintballing) will require fees for trips and equipment.

Most universities will have some sort of film society. If one doesn't exist consider creating one with others on your course as this is a great way to meet like-minded people who share a passion for film. Within the society you can meet up and put together programmes with all sorts of films, go to the cinema as a group, and even organise trips to premieres or film festivals. If a film society exists at your university, you could also consider creating a new society that revolves around a particular type of film, such as a horror movie club, or a Dogme appreciation film society. Before deciding to create a society, make sure that you find out all the relevant information from the Student Union.

MONEY

Money is an aspect that will have a profound effect on your life at university, especially if you have moved away from home. You will now be in control of things such as buying food and paying rent. For many students, this may be your first time where you will have to manage money-related issues. A student loan will probably be your first source of income. Student loans are paid in instalments, allowing for the more frivolous to still have money if they spend most of their loan at once. Unlike regular loans, student loans are exactly that, loans specifically designed for students, so they do not come with the high interest rate charges that loan companies are notorious for.

To apply for your student loan you will receive a booklet to fill in with information such as bank details, your university and parental income to help to determine how much you will receive. It is best to fill this in as soon as possible to ensure that you receive your loan at the start of your first semester. This will also give you time to change any mistakes or provide further information.

BUDGETING

Budgeting is a very important factor at university; although it may take a while until you have sorted out a practical, balanced budget from which you can live. Creating a budget will mean that you don't have to struggle in the last few weeks before the next instalment of your loan arrives.

■   Make sure you put money aside for essentials such as rent and bills; if they go unpaid you can find yourself in trouble.
■   Write a brief list of what necessities you will have to take into account such as food. Try and work out a reasonable amount to spend (this may mean that you will not be able to buy as many luxury treats, but this will give you more money to spend elsewhere).
■   Once you have decided on a budget make a note of your outgoings; this way you can see if your budget is working for you.
■   Try not to get too bogged down with money worries. At the end of your degree you are likely to be in debt even if you are careful with money. You are allowed to enjoy yourself, just remember to be sensible.

The thing to remember when creating a budget is that everyone will be different depending on their circumstances and likes and dislikes, but don't be off put by other people's spending. If you stick to a set budget you will be able to enjoy your university experience and still be able to afford to occasionally buy luxury items without having to go without food or clean clothes.

FOOD SHOPPING

If you have moved away from home to live at university then this may be one of the first times that you will have to buy and cook your own food. This may seem like a chore but what you eat can

21

have a great effect on your moods and your health. Also what you decide to buy can have a great effect on your wallet.

Tips for new students:

■ Don't dismiss supermarkets' own brands or value ranges; they may be a step down from the leading brands, but so is the price.

■ If cooking isn't your strong point don't rely on 'Ready Meals' alone, as they can be expensive and not very nutritious; it could be useful to learn to make a few simple meals.

■ Keep a look out for offers such as 'buy one get one free'; they can save you a lot of money and usually include more expensive products so you can afford to treat yourself.

■ Many supermarkets will reduce items in the evenings, meaning you can pick up some cheap products, yet it is important to eat them before the sell-by date expires.

■ Try to eat a good range of foods so you don't get bored with the food you eat.

■ Eating with friends once in a while can be cost-effective and you may also learn some new recipes.

■ Eating out and takeaways can provide a hassle-free meal; however, they do cost a lot; try not to get them too often; the price of one pizza could buy you a lot more from a supermarket.

■ If you choose to order a takeaway, then look for special student offers on menus.

PART-TIME WORK

Part-time employment is a common way to achieve a steady income whilst at university and is a necessity for many students. Part-time work can provide a break from university life and also allow you to create another social circle. However . . .

- It is important that you dictate the hours that you are willing to work. Employers obviously do not think of your university commitments, and may try to make you do too many hours.
- If you do get a job, you might want to think of cutting down your hours close to hand-in dates, so that you can dedicate more time to your work.
- Be aware that some jobs may require you to work during Easter and Christmas breaks, meaning that you may not be able to go home over the holiday period, so make sure you ask about this.
- Don't let your part-time job become your main priority; see it as a way to earn extra cash to fund your degree so that you do not let your course work suffer.

WORK EXPERIENCE

Work experience can be a great idea while you are at university. It will allow you to gain vital experience which can help you decide exactly what you want to do once you have graduated. Work experience can help you when applying for future jobs. Film Studies is a very popular subject which means that there is a lot of competition for jobs, so many employers will want the most experienced candidates. The best thing to do when it comes to finding work experience is to start looking early on and use all the avenues at your disposal, such as the internet, newspapers, careers advisors and general enquiries. By using many resources you will provide yourself with the best possible chance of finding something to suit you.

When you come to university and the subject of careers comes up the buzzword you will often hear is 'networking'. Networking is about trying to gain experience in the industry by getting to know a large number of people. A good way to achieve this is to speak to people and join in as much as possible while at your placement so that you are remembered. Keeping in contact with people in the industry could lead to further opportunities.

23

If you are having trouble finding work experience, don't get too downhearted. The film industry is a competitive market so you may have to do a lot of searching and make many enquiries before you find a placement. The main thing to remember is that any experience is good experience. Many of the more competitive placements such as trainee positions will more often that not require experienced candidates so the more experience you have the better. Even when a placement is not your ideal choice, it could lead to bigger and better things, some useful contacts, and will look good on your C.V.

If you are stuck for ideas when looking for placements, consider the following:

- Trainee positions at the BBC.
- Runners in the areas of film, television or music videos.
- Work experience positions for film publications at national and local level.
- Work experience for local newspapers or magazines.
- Employment opportunities within your university departments (guides for Open Days, film-making opportunities, administrative work, etc.)

CONCLUSION

Overall, the initial transition to university can be daunting but you will soon adapt to the lifestyle and responsibilities that come with it. University will be one of the best times of you life, but make sure you balance your work and play so that at the end of it you leave with many memories and a well-earned degree.

Chapter 4

Lecture and seminar skills

Ruth Doughty and Deborah Shaw

PREPARATION FOR DISCUSSION

What are your expectations of lectures and seminars? Do you have any worries? What do you hope to learn from them? What is your role? What is the role of the lecturer?

INTRODUCTION

Learning in higher education can be very different to previous learning experiences. While at school and college the information imparted in classes is often geared towards passing exams. In written work, you will mainly rely on the information given by teachers as you are not expected to consult many other sources. At university, an hour's lecture or seminar is simply an introduction to the subject, and you are expected to use this as a stepping stone for your own detailed research.

PREPARATION FOR LECTURES AND SEMINARS

It is a good idea to be aware of what you are about to study. This can be achieved by watching a film in advance related to the topic. For example, if you have a lecture on Dogme 95, why not watch one of the key films associated with the Danish film movement. If the set text is Von Trier's *The Idiots* (1998) you could also watch *Festen* (Thomas Vinterberg, 1998). This means that you will be familiar with the stylistic traits and as a result you will gain more from the lecture. It is also beneficial to do some background reading on the topic in advance as this will help you to understand the information given.

ETIQUETTE

There are some forms of behaviour that are expected of you at lectures and seminars: here is a type of unwritten code between lecturers and students. Try to adhere to the following:

- Arrive at least five minutes before the lecture/seminar is about to begin – it makes a very poor impression on the lecturer if you are late and can also disturb your fellow students.
- Keep an open mind about what to expect from the lecture; some seemingly dull topics may be surprisingly interesting.
- Make sure you are well equipped with materials you may need (handbook, pens, paper, etc.).
- Remember to turn off your mobile phone.
- Don't chat to your friends. It is distracting for other students and the lecturer.
- If the lecturer chooses to ask a question, do not be afraid to attempt an answer. It doesn't matter if you make a mistake.
- If you are unable to attend a lecture or seminar then it is polite to contact the unit lecturer/tutor/administrator to inform them.

LECTURES

Lectures are a way of imparting knowledge to a large group of students. Your lecturer will often have spent weeks or even months preparing a topic. It will be a condensed summary of key concepts and academic ideas. Therefore, it is important to attend lectures and to ensure that you gain as much as you can from them.

Lecturing is the traditional format used at universities. Because it is so traditional it can often be regarded as quite an archaic, old-fashioned form of learning. However, attending lectures should never be a passive experience, especially when studying film. Most film lectures will include illustrative clips and the experience on the whole can be both informative and entertaining.

NOTE-TAKING TIPS

As time progresses you will develop you own style of note-taking. However, initially, the whole process can be quite daunting. It is assumed that will just know what to do at your first lecture, but this isn't always the case. Should you write down everything or nothing? What do you do with terms that are new to you? Below you will find some useful advice:

■ Do not try to reproduce the lecturer's every word. Try to rephrase words and capture the key concepts without getting bogged down with jargon and academic terminology.

■ Try to make your notes coherent.

■ Do not become a PowerPoint zombie. Be aware of what you are writing rather than copying PowerPoint slides verbatim.

■ Listen to what is being said whilst you are taking notes otherwise you may overlook some key facts.

■ Make sure you collect any handouts and also find out whether there is any supplementary material provided online.

■ Don't worry about getting the full details of a film, e.g. the director's name and year, if you are rushing; you can always look this up on www.imdb.com following the lecture.

■ Rather than switch off when clips are shown, make sure you write down the name of the film in case you want to refer to it in an assignment. Also make a note of any interesting formal elements.

■ It is best that you read over your notes while the lecture is still fresh in your mind. You may want to rewrite them to make them clearer, highlight significant points or produce a more in-depth version for revision purposes.

■ Write down any questions you may have. You can always ask the lecturer at the end of the session or ask your tutor to address any queries in your seminars. Alternatively, you can use these questions to guide your independent study.

■ Remember to write down all the films that relate to the specific topic. When it comes to writing your assignment it is good to refer to a broad range of filmic sources.

ABBREVIATIONS

You will be familiar with abbreviations from text-messaging on your mobile phones. You can find abbreviating words a useful technique when taking notes.

Here are some film-related and other examples.

Hollywood	Hwd
Black and White	b+w
Director	dir.
French New Wave	Fr NW
Italian Neo-realism	It NR
German Expressionism	Germ Ex
British	Brit
American	Am
European	Euro
Industry	Ind
Government	Gvt
Production	Prod

Company	Co.
Censorship	Cens
Editing/Editor/Edit	Ed.
Mise-en-scène	Mise
Resulted/caused/meant	=
Lead to/followed	›
In addition/furthermore	+

A common problem with note-taking is that you can try to write too much and not be able to keep up with the lecturer. Below is an example of what the lecturer said, followed by an example of a short-hand version:

> As a result of Stalinist intervention in the Russian film industry, not only were completed films censored and repressed, but the actual scripts and production of films were kept under close government scrutiny.

Your notes could read:

> Stalin (gvt) = all film prod censored incl. scripts

SEMINAR EXERCISE

Can you think of any useful abbreviations that could be used in note-taking?

SEMINARS

Seminars are a crucial part of your learning experience. While they may appear to be an optional part of the programme, they are actually a key component to any degree. Seminars provide you with the opportunity to raise any questions and concerns regarding material covered in the lecture. They are also a forum in which you can explore the topic in greater depth, focusing on a specific film text or reading. Seminars generally take the form of smaller groups (10–30 people); this gives you the opportunity to talk and to get to know other people on your courses. Whether the class is good or not depends largely on you as well as the lecturer. All seminars require is a little preparation and a willingness to talk.

Seminars provide an arena which is peer-focused and will typically be more informal than lectures, allowing you to experiment with your own ideas and share them with your fellow students. As such, there are no wrong answers and you should feel encouraged to talk freely. This is the place to raise any concerns if you are struggling with any concepts covered in either the lecture or the reading. The worst thing you can do is to remain silent.

6 SEMINAR COMMANDMENTS

The following are some rules guiding seminar participation:

- In order to get the most from the seminar experience it is vital that you contribute to discussions.
- Don't be afraid to test out ideas, even if you are unsure of whether they work.
- Do not monopolise class discussions – let everyone have a chance to speak. Be prepared to listen.
- Do not let attendance slip.
- Be supportive to other students in your group.
- Make sure you have watched the set film or read the set text in advance. To attend class without doing the specific tasks just wastes everybody's time.

SEMINAR EXERCISE

'This ice breaking seminar . . .' exercise is based on the memory game 'I went to the shops and I bought . . . .' This version is entitled 'I went to the cinema and I saw . . . .' You must also express whether you liked or disliked the film. The next student must repeat what was said previously and then add their own version.

I went to the cinema and I saw *Moulin Rouge* and I loved it.
    Jenny went to the cinema and saw *Moulin Rouge* and loved it. I went to the cinema and saw *Lord of the Rings* and hated it.
    Jenny went to the cinema and saw *Moulin Rouge* and loved it. Duncan went to the cinema and saw *Lord of the Rings* and hated it. I went to the cinema and saw *Casablanca* and loved it.

REFLECTION

- How did you feel about having to speak in class?
- Did the fact that everyone had to speak help?
- Did you enjoy the exercise or not?
- What was the role of the tutor?

Chapter 5

The library: the lecturer's perspective

Justin Smith

READING

Prior to the plenary session organised by the library, make sure that you have read the following introduction.

One of your early tasks in the heady first days and weeks of university life is to become acquainted with the library. True, it may not be near the top of your list of priorities once Freshers' Week is over. But whether you are a bibliophobe or a bookworm, sooner or later the university library is going to be essential to your success on the degree course. Why?

- All intellectual enquiry depends upon an awareness of the field of study.
- In an academic environment we are required to substantiate (not merely reiterate) our own views by referring to primary and secondary sources of evidence.
- In humanities-based subjects at least, most written (and some oral) assessment activities require engagement with critical views and debates from published sources (books, journals, electronic texts, the internet).

■ We can usually gain a lot from an understanding of some established writing on a particular theme.

However, deciding where to start can at first be daunting. Introductory guides, library tours, online catalogues and advice from the library staff can all be helpful. But once you've found what you are looking for, some questions still remain.

HOW MANY SOURCES SHOULD I USE?

■ On some common topics (genre, let's say, or a particular national cinema) there may be copious literature. Weighing-up the alternatives will be the issue here.
■ Narrower subjects might rely on one key text (of which there may be multiple copies).

There is not a simple answer to this question. Seek advice from relevant lecturers, unit handbooks and library staff on the particular topic you are researching. However, a bibliography with only one or even two key texts is not considered satisfactory at university level.

HOW DO I TELL WHICH ARE THE BEST TEXTS?

Again, recommendations regarding books and journal articles from staff and course reading lists are a useful guide.

■ Where a range of sources is available, check out the most recent first (finding its publication date in your handbook, in the library catalogue or in the book or journal).
■ For a summary of content, consult the publisher's blurb on the back or the journal abstract and skim through the author's bibliography. Are there prior works on the same subject referenced there? Does the library hold these too?

- As a rough guide you can expect the most recent academic work to be the most up-to-date (in that the author will probably have read all the major existing literature on the subject), but that doesn't necessarily make it the most authoritative source.
- On a practical level, once you've selected your sources, decide which you can (or need to) borrow (and for how long), and what you are able to copy from or photocopy in the library before you leave (bearing in mind copyright regulations).

DO I NEED TO USE DIFFERENT KINDS OF SOURCES?

You'll learn quickly that the different types of sources available via the library and elsewhere can be categorised in several ways.

- You'll find books on film texts and genres, film directors, stars, national film industries, film theories and audiences.
- Some will offer surveys, debates and particular perspectives, while others may be encyclopaedic and mainly for reference.
- Most books and anthologies on topics connected with film are written by scholars, as are many articles to be found in a wide variety of periodicals (another name for journals).

A good tip is to find out which cinema journals your library keeps and to be aware of their academic status.

- Some, like *Screen* or the *Historical Journal of Radio, Film and Television*, are resolutely academic.
- Others (such as *Sight and Sound*) might be described as middle-of-the-road: serious, often scholarly criticism, but presented in a 'newsy', review-based, magazine format. Typically they might include contributions from journalists and critics, as well as academics.

35

■ At the other end of the spectrum are popular film magazines like *Empire* and *Total Film*. Though they may be written in a popular style to suit their particular target audience, such publications can tell us something about the current film scene, audience tastes and fan cultures. If you are investigating contemporary cinema reception, these might be useful sources. Otherwise, as a rule, they are not acceptable as academic references for interpreting film.

This leads us to two important principles by which to evaluate sources.

■ Firstly, what type of source is this, who is it written by and for whom?
■ And secondly, how relevant are its contents to the topic or issue I am researching?

These simple criteria can be applied equally to internet sources, though in the case of the world wide web they can sometimes be harder to answer.

■ Try to find (via your library's electronic databases) reputable on-line sources (such as the FIAF or the Film Index International) for more reliable information about cinema.
■ As with popular magazines, fan websites can reveal much about fans (if that's your interest), but don't rely on them for your definition of Eisensteinian montage!

It may appear from this judgement that there exist hierarchies of sources. This is true, but it's not a matter simply of snobbery. It is about two things: reliability and relevance. With experience, you will be able to judge these for yourself. In the meantime, take the advice of lecturers and library staff. In practice, a balance of sources is best. The internet on its own is not enough!

HOW DO I MAKE SENSE OF WHAT I'VE READ?

As in all things, practice makes perfect. But the best principle is to adopt an organised, systematic approach to assimilating resources.

- When you have found a likely text, first of all make a note of its bibliographical details (author, title, publisher, year, page references, library shelf no.). This is not only a sensible method of cataloguing what you have read; it will save you time when compiling your bibliography.
- Then use the cover blurb, contents page and perhaps the preface or introduction to get the gist of the territory covered. It may be that a particular chapter will be most relevant to your work. A book's index can be useful here.
- So, the technique is to scan and skim-read for relevance, then focus-in on key sections for in-depth reading. In practice only rarely is there either time or necessity to read a whole book cover to cover!
- Make sure to preface your notes on a particularly useful section of a source with its keywords, major topics or distinctive ideas. One major advantage of photocopied material (from books or journals) is that you can use highlighter pens or underlining to do this.
- Topic headings will help as an aide-memoire to identify each source you have used. And keep these notes for future reference, even when the current assignment is done.
- Efficient researchers often compile card index systems (either on paper or pc) to catalogue what they've read. In this way, during your three-year degree, you will amass your own personal 'library' of key film texts. And you'll be surprised how many you return to time and again – they become the touchstones of your learning.

WHAT IF ALL THE BOOKS HAVE GONE?

We have shared an assumption about the ideal library which in practice does not always exist. In the best-stocked university library, with a film section to rival the BFI, there will be bottlenecks at assessment-time when key works are all on loan. There is no magic solution to this fact of student life – only some potential ways around it.

- The first piece of advice is to think ahead. As soon as unit handbooks or study materials are handed out take a look at the reading lists (which the subject librarian should also have) and identify likely key texts. Get hold of these well in advance.
- Use the library catalogue to ascertain where there are multiple copies of a popular text whether some are available on short-loan terms.
- Find out about your library's procedures for reserving titles and for interlibrary loans. Both facilities can be useful, but again, they need to be arranged in advance.
- Where there are obvious choices in assessment topics, let the available resources be your guide.
- Consider electronic texts, internet resources and photocopiable journal articles as ready alternatives to borrowing books. They may require a bit further digging, but they can be just as useful, and more readily available, than high-demand books.
- Most university libraries are repositories of untold riches. But unearthing their treasures depends upon the resourcefulness of the student as well.

SEMINAR EXERCISE

1   Produce a half-page note summary of key advice in the reading above, as an aide-memoire to visiting the library.

2   Imagine you are given an assignment to write a film review of the recent Bond film *Casino Royale* (Campbell, 2006). What sources (give types and titles) would it be best to consult? Which of them would you find in the library, and where?

3   Find out the library catalogue shelf mark for film resources. Then, when you visit the library, find out where these shelves are.

4   How many items are you allowed to borrow from the library? What is not available for loan?

5   The library catalogue may provide book titles and author names in response to keyword searches, but that's of little help when consulting journals. How do you search these?

6   For an end-of-semester assignment you are asked to write a 2000-word essay on Classical Hollywood Narrative. You have been given a reading list. Which titles would you go to first? How many do you think you should consult to produce a well-informed essay?

Chapter 6

The library: the librarian's perspective

David Francis and Greta Friggens

INTRODUCTION

Today's university libraries are much more than buildings housing books and journals. These are, of course, still essential tools for research, but changes in learning and teaching methods and the way you want to study are clearly reflected in the way libraries have developed. More and more resources are becoming easily accessible through the internet including academic books and journals. You can access your files and undertake research when and wherever is convenient to you. Within the library itself, there are spaces for a range of different study activities, from group work to the more traditional individual, silent study. Wireless connections and IT areas enable you to use the space in all sorts of different ways. Cafés and social zones are often part of the learning space too.

LIBRARIANS

People who work in libraries, from the most junior assistant up to the boss him or herself, have one major priority and that is to help their customers. Your university library may well be bigger than anything you've encountered before; perhaps at first glance it's somewhat intimidating. But no apologies for repeating, all members of the library staff are there to help you to do as much as you can to maximise your achievements on your course. Some are

41

more experienced in certain areas than others; many will have degrees and further qualifications. There is probably a subject librarian in your area who works closely with the academic staff in your department. That person is likely to meet you, formally, at different stages of your course to help you to develop skills in finding, using and evaluating information in its many forms. Informally, they are usually happy to discuss your information concerns at any stage of your course, so do seek them out if you need help. There is a lot more to a university library than an optimistic wander around the shelves in the hope of finding something useful. An ever-increasing amount of information is available virtually, so ensure that you explore the library's web pages and see what is available from the student portal and VLE (Virtual Learning Environment) too.

NAVIGATION

So, where will the film studies books be? Try not to think of there being just one section of the library where all 'your' books are. From your previous use of libraries, you'll know that the books have a shelfmark or classmark – numbers and/or letters at the bottom of the spine. Think of this as a code standing for the subject of the book. Many libraries use the Dewey Decimal classification, named after its inventor, the American librarian Melvil Dewey (1851–1931). Most public and university libraries in this country use it, and many take their catalogue records from a central source, so a great deal of commonality is found. Anything in the section 791.43 . . . will have something to do with Film Studies. You'll probably find most numbers are longer than this, subdividing the topic into, for example, books about film history, books about particular directors and actors, film genres, national cinemas and so on. Which section of the library you should be using really depends on what you are researching at any given time. Here are just a few areas that may be of interest:

791.43	**film studies**
791.4309	cinema history
791.435	film genre
791.45	television
302.23	**media studies**
302.2343	film/cinema
302.2345	television
808.2	**drama**
808.22	scriptwriting for television
808.23	scriptwriting for film

Some university libraries use the Library of Congress classification scheme. Where this is the case, the most likely area to find Film Studies material is around PN 3295, and the same caveats apply as to some of the examples above.

How do you find out if the library has the books you want, or how do you find out if the library has any books on a particular subject? The key to any library's collection is its catalogue. There will almost certainly be dedicated terminals in the library and it will also be accessible via the internet (as indeed are the catalogues of most university and public libraries – handy for checking out what's available locally when you are at home in the vacations).

To begin with, you are likely to need to check for items on a reading list or from a course handbook. Some university libraries have online reading list services where you can link straight from the reading list into the library catalogue. However, often you will have to start with the library catalogue.

As a general rule, when using a library catalogue, 'less is more'. If you are confronted with a screen that looks like the following example don't try to fill in all the boxes; just the author's last name and a few words from the start of the title will do. Many catalogues now have a free text search box, so again, keep your search simple.

If you don't find what you are looking for at the first attempt, then try again; perhaps just try searching for the author.

Author:

Title:

Keyword:

If the catalogue finds some results relating to your search, follow the links until you see as much information as you need to locate the book. This will include the details of:

The location of the book	Especially important if your university has several libraries. Often location indicates a virtual or electronic book, 'e-book'.
Special collections	This refers to books on short loan or rare books.
The full shelfmark or classmark	Usually this is the Dewey number, followed by some filing letters, e.g. 791.43 WAL. There will be lots of books filed at this number, but fewer with the same filing letters.

Your reading list is only a selection of what is available in the library. Remember that all of the other people on your course will have that same reading list, so you will be expected to carry out some of your own research too. Try this exercise to get a feel for what is available in your library.

SEMINAR EXERCISE

1 Try out a keyword search on gender and film.

 Tip: if you have been set an essay question, choose one of two key words from the question and remember that you may have to think of alternative words which may be more specific or less so, e.g. women and Hollywood.

2 How many titles match your search?

3 Can you can sort your search results, e.g. by date?

 Tip: this can be useful if you have a long list of results as it allows you to see what has been published most recently, at the top.

4 Refer to the list above. Does the screen showing your search results give you all the information you need to find the book on the shelf?

5 If necessary, click on any further links and make a note of the full details you will need to locate the book.

6 Now use any maps and plans of your library to locate the sections you need.

 Tip: always ask for help if you don't find what you need; library staff can often identify reasons why the book is not where it should be, for instance, it might be waiting to be re-shelved.

ACCESSING BOOKS

University libraries aren't expected to provide one copy of every book on every reading list for every student on every course. There will be times when all the copies of the book you are looking for are on loan. Make sure you are the next to get it when it comes back. Many systems give you the facility to reserve an item on loan there and then, so check what your library's practice on recalling books for reservations is. Another frequently found facility is to be able to renew loans from the screen. Again, if in doubt, get a member of staff to show you how it's done. Remember that all this is likely to be possible from the internet.

You may find that your library has different loan periods for different types of books. Many have the basic course textbooks in short loan collections, for example. These may be located in a separate room where you can either browse or request what you need. Typically, such items can only be borrowed for one day or even a few hours. But remember that you don't always need to read a book all the way through; a chapter here or there is often sufficient for your purposes (like that essay that's due in tomorrow).

Many libraries have a collection of reference books, often shelved somewhere different from where the books available for loan are. Don't overlook reference books, dictionaries, encyclopaedias and the like. For example, if you are dealing for the first time with a director you know nothing about, the short entry in something like the *International Dictionary of Films and Filmmakers; directors* [Detroit, London: St James Press, (4th edn), 2000] will probably provide a useful starting point before you try to tackle something more substantial.

A fast-developing field is the provision of electronic books that is making available the full text of books, including reference books, to your computer. While reading from a screen is not as pleasant as reading a traditional book, the instant availability of a popular title is a big bonus. Available titles and means of access may vary in different institutions. Here is yet another service where you may find the guidance of a member of your library's staff helpful.

JOURNALS

Your library may call this collection journals, periodicals or serials; essentially they are magazine-like publications that are devoted to a particular topic. They appear at fixed intervals, weekly, monthly or quarterly, and contain articles written by practitioners or academics and often contain cutting-edge research. Your library is bound to have a number of film-related titles. Sometimes they are all shelved in a separate area from the books, sometimes they are given class-marks and shelved with or near the books on the same subjects. If you already have an A-level in Film or Media Studies, you may well have encountered *Sight and Sound*. There are many other journals relating to film studies, including *American Cinematographer*; *Film Comment*; *Film Quarterly*; *Historical Journal of Film, Radio and Television*; *Journal of British Cinema and Television*; *Screen*; and *Studies in European Cinema*.

SIGHT AND SOUND EXERCISE

1   If your library catalogue has a title search box, type *Sight and Sound* in the box.

2   Look out for an option which will enable you to limit your search to a specific collection. Choose journals, periodicals or serials if you can.

 (If your library catalogue has a single search box, you may be able to limit your search when the initial results have been found.)

3   If your library subscribes to *Sight and Sound*, the catalogue will show you details of the years and volumes held by your library.

 Tip: if this is not obvious from the page you are looking at, follow the links until you can see the details.

4   Make a note of the following details:

 ■   Location, e.g. the site where the journal is held (of relevance in universities where there is more than one library).
 ■   Shelfmark details.
 ■   Years held by your library – note older volumes may be in a different location to current issues.

> Tip: If you see a date, followed by a hyphen, e.g. 1984–, this means that your library has volumes from 1984 right up to the current issue.
>
> ■ Is there a link to an electronic edition? This may be the only means of accessing the journal.
>
> Go and find where *Sight and Sound* is located in your library. It is important to note that all the content for specific years is available in an annual index. Locate the index for 2008 and identify items that are of interest to you.

Library staff frequently get enquiries about finding journals and searching their contents, so don't be afraid to ask for help. It is vital that you familiarise yourself with what is available.

Journals frequently contain cutting-edge and up-to-date research, and can be a very useful source for your studies. Remember the most recent edition of a journal may be on display, rather than catalogued with the other journals. An advantage to using journals is that they are always available, as most universities do not allow you to take them off-site. In addition, you will often find reviews of films that have not yet made it into any book, or indeed aren't destined to get a mention in a book at all.

You might be wondering how you find a specific item in a journal. Library catalogues rarely index the contents of journals held in the library. So here's where we meet online *databases* – large indexes of references to articles, published in lots of different journals. The means of getting access to these may well differ from library to library, and whether you are 'on campus' or at your computer. The library staff can easily show you how it's done, and how to search them successfully.

Databases such as *Film Index International* or *FIAF International Film Archive* will enable you to search for information about a particular film, person or topic relating to the industry. As with searching the library catalogue to find books, you will need to think carefully about which key words will produce the most relevant results. The results will give you enough information to locate the article either from your library or from another. Often, you will be given some more detail including an abstract (summary of the article) to help you decide whether you want to read it.

Here is a fictional example of how your search results might be presented:

AUTHOR	Helsing, Thomas van.
TITLE	The vampire films of the Wiltshire Studios.
SOURCE	*Journal of Cinematic Necrology*, vol. 4, no. 3, September 2001, pp. 106–16.
ABSTRACT	The films *The Galloping Ghoul* and *The Bulgarian Bloodsucker* are discussed in some depth. Briefly considers several other offerings from the same studio; short interview with the director, Jonathan Westenra.
SUBJECTS	Vampire films; Wiltshire Studios; Westenra, Jonathan.

How do I know if the article is available in the library? Check the source details on your library catalogue; in this instance you would search for the fictitious *Journal of Cinematic Necrology*. Make sure that your library has the correct volume in stock. Often you will notice a 'locate full text' or 'article linker' button which will enable you to automatically link to an electronic version of the article, if it is available.

If the article is not available from your library, you can usually obtain it through an inter-library loan service. Ask library staff or visit your library web pages for further information.

More and more libraries are subscribing to whole collections of journals that are available electronically. Ask library staff about such services as JSTOR and EBSCO. The number of Film Studies journals available is constantly expanding. It's extremely useful to be able to sit at your own computer and browse or search the contents of a number of journals, and then call up the article.

The range of resources available will vary from library to library, so it is important that you get to know what is available in your institutions. Libraries usually produce guides on using their services and many of the online resources also provide tutorials which will help you use them effectively. You may find these useful but, if you are given the opportunity to attend formal sessions on using library resources effectively, do make the most of the opportunity. You may think that you know all there is to know about using libraries when you arrive at university, or you may think that the answers are all out there on the web. In reality, resources and tools for accessing information are constantly changing and developing, so if you are serious about your course of study and being an information-literate member of society, then libraries and librarians are your allies. They are there to help you succeed.

Chapter 8

Reading skills

Ruth Doughty and Deborah Shaw

INTRODUCTION

There is a common misconception that Film Studies students spend all day watching films and rarely set foot in a library. However, in addition to reading visual information, reading books and articles are at the root of your learning experience at university. Written material is at the very heart of all academic studies. To have a deep understanding of your discipline, you need to familiarise yourself with the key literature for any topic that you are studying. You cannot, at this level, rely purely on the information given to you in lectures. To do well in your assignments, you must demonstrate evidence that you have read the work of scholars who are specialists in the field. Lecturers do not want to read regurgitated material taken from their lectures.

Most of what you will learn on your Film Studies degree will come from directed reading. You will have access to many excellent resources in your library, and the amount of reading that you are expected to do can appear overwhelming. It is worth noting that there is a lot of reading you don't have to do. What we mean by this is that you will receive a reading list for each unit, but you will not be expected to read every book on the list as you won't have time. You are also not expected to read every word of every book and need to learn how to be selective.

The amount of reading that you are required to do depends on the nature of each unit. Film Theory, for example, will involve a great deal of reading, while the more practical units may not be text-based. Make sure that you know what is expected of you in terms of set readings, and secondary sources. Ensure that you have access to all the materials and prepare any readings in good time.

PREPARING FOR YOUR READING

Ways of reading have changed dramatically in recent times with the development of online resources. Whereas traditionally academics would spend a considerable amount of time in archives and specialist libraries, nowadays much of this information is available online. This means that you can carry out preliminary research into what is available before you physically arrive in the library.

Therefore, one of the ways in which you can help to focus your reading is to be aware of the material that is going to be useful for your research. Instead of spending a great deal of unproductive time searching through the library catalogue and shelves, it is a good idea to investigate key texts on the internet beforehand. There are a number of sites which allow you to look at both the contents and indexes of books. In particular, the American Amazon.com website (and to some extent the UK-based Amazon.co.uk) provides a 'Search Inside' facility. This allows you access to digitally scanned images of the 'Table of Contents', the 'Index' and frequently sample chapters. From these images you will be able to assess whether specific books will be of use for your research. Doing this kind of preliminary preparation will mean that you know exactly which books/articles to get from the library – you will also know the exact chapters and pages that will be most helpful. Additionally, there is Google Books, which also grants you permission to look at a significant proportion of the contents of many books.

FOLLOW UP ACTIVITY

Go on to Google Books, and do a search for a term relating to one of your assignments.

- How many results are returned?
- How many books will be of use?
- How much information are you able to access?
- Which of these resources are available from your library?

Be prepared to report back to the class with your findings.

READING ONLINE

Most institutions provide access to electronic books. Depending on which companies your university subscribes to, you may find links to one or all of the following providers: Ebrary, My I Library, and Net Library. These facilities allow you to access and read books online from your own computer. Most of these providers include additional functions, for example, you can search the text for key terms; you may be able to highlight areas of particular interest; you can make detailed notes which will then be sent to your email account; you may find links to dictionaries in case you come across any new terms that you are unfamiliar with. In short, it is worth exploring the functions of each of these electronic providers to see what they offer you.

READING TIPS

Whether you are following a traditional format or utilising online resources, the following guidelines will help organise and structure your reading activities at university:

- Make sure that you start reading early in the semester.
- Don't leave your reading until the last minute as it is a time-consuming activity.
- Follow up lectures with a visit to the library to do some additional reading on the topic.
- Don't try to read if you are tired as it is hard to concentrate.
- Take breaks when you need them.
- Make sure that your reading is focused and relates to the topic that you are studying or to your essay question.
- Decide on the importance of the material and whether it is worth reading carefully or whether you should skim read.
- Question what the author is saying and make a note of your response. Good researchers are prepared to take on established ideas, and are not afraid to disagree with the critics.
- Look up terms that you don't understand in a dictionary, and note their meaning.
- It is a good idea to have a film reference book at hand to help with any terms that you are unsure of. We recommend Hayward, S. (2006) *Cinema Studies: The Key Concepts* (3rd edn), London: Routledge.
- Be prepared to read around the subject; this will greatly improve your understanding of the topic.
- Discuss the readings with friends on the course. This can be beneficial if you have struggled with any concepts in the reading.
- You may have to read an article/chapter more than once to fully understand it.

SEMINAR EXERCISE

In class read the preface in this book written by Sue Harper and discuss the following questions:

1 How long did it take you? Did you change speed at any point and why?

2 How many of the key points can you recall?

3 Did you highlight or underline anything on the page?

4 Did you take any notes?

5 Were you able to concentrate? What are your ideal reading conditions?

NOTE-TAKING WHEN READING

Note-taking is basically used to help you remember key aspects of your readings and is useful for revision purposes. It is important not to be passive in your reading; active note-taking will help you digest and understand the information. Here is some useful advice that will guide your note-taking.

■ Photocopy the most relevant readings and then you can underline, highlight and add notes in the margins.

■ Highlight or underline central ideas and any key quotations that will be useful for your essays.

■ Never write notes or make any markings in the books, unless they are your personal property.

■ Don't take too many notes. Just focus on the key points. It can be very hard to write an essay from pages and pages of notes.

■ Use your own words. This not only helps you to grasp the key points, but also reduces the risk of any inadvertent plagiarism.

■ Always note down the reference details (the author, year of publication, book/article title, place of publication, publisher and page number). You will need this information for correct referencing.

■ Organise your notes into whatever format suits you (spider diagram, flow chart etc.).

SEMINAR EXERCISE

Reread the preface and fill in the following chart. You can bear these headings in mind for any other readings you may do.

Key Ideas	
Useful references	
Unfamiliar terminology	
Criticisms or disagreements with author	
Questions	

Chapter 9

Online research and resources

Ruth Doughty

INTRODUCTION

The internet is probably the greatest resource available to students and academics. It has dramatically changed the way that all of us approach academic work, and the key to effective research is knowing how to navigate your way around the information highway. There is so much material on line, and this can often be daunting. This chapter attempts to provide some helpful advice to make the most of web-based resources.

SEARCH ENGINES

The world-wide web is a vast resource of URLs (uniform resource locators, also known as web addresses) and hyperlinked documents, images and other resources. As a student it is important that you are able to navigate your way around the web in order to access information that is both relevant and academically reliable. Developing your search skills is one of the best ways of avoiding many of the poor resources found on the net.

There are two different types of search engines available to you when trying to locate resources on the internet.

- General search engines
- Meta-search engines

General search engines: These are the day-to-day individual search engines that most people are familiar with. The best-known examples include: Google, Yahoo, AltaVista and Ask.com

Meta-search engines: Here your request is simultaneously sent to a number of individual search engines. Meta-search engines do not own a collection of web pages but have the facility to send your enquiry to databases held by a number of different individual search engines. Examples include: Dogpile, Excite and Metacrawler.

BOOLEAN LOGIC AND OTHER TIPS

One of the best ways of refining your enquiry, when looking for information on the internet, is through the inclusion of quotation marks. For example when searching for the movie mogul Jack Warner, if you type **Jack Warner** into the Google search box 682,000 results are returned. If you now repeat this exercise but insert **"Jack Warner"** with the inclusion of the quotation marks the number of results is considerably reduced to 241,000.

Boolean logic is a great way to help finely tune your ability to search the Internet. Named after the mathematician George Boole, Boolean logic is a way of refining your search through the inclusion of the following three Boolean operators:

- OR
- AND / +
- NOT / −

Using these keywords (operators) will help you filter the information that is retrieved from your enquiry, as the following Venn diagram illustrates.

Similarly you can insert a star symbol (asterisk) as a wild card. For example, if you cannot find the name of a director but know the title of a film you could try typing the following:

ET was directed by *
Moulin Rouge was directed by *

The search results for the first query should correctly identify Steven Spielberg as the director. However, the results for *Moulin Rouge* are somewhat confusing as there seems to be a number of directors associated with this film; Baz Luhrmann (2001), John Huston (1952) and John Renoir (1954) all appear in the results. This is because all of the above directors have made a film taking the Moulin Rouge as its subject. Interestingly, Renoir's film about the notorious Parisian nightclub was called *French Cancan* (1954), yet the internet correctly identified the film as relevant.

SEMINAR EXERCISE

Try the following exercises either in class or at home. Note the difference Boolean logic, and the use of asterisks and quotation marks, makes to the results that are returned.

Keyword	No. of results
Michael Powell	
"Michael Powell"	
Emeric Pressburger	
"Emeric Pressburger"	
Michael Powell AND Emeric Pressburger	
Michael Powell NOT Emeric Pressburger	
Michael Powell OR Emeric Pressburger	
"Peeping Tom" was directed by *	

69

TRUSTWORTHY SITES

As a young academic, one of the most difficult problems you will face is deciding whether the information you find on the internet is of a good scholarly standard or alternatively, populist writing. At some point in your degree you may be asked to assess fan-based writing (web ethnography), but it is important that you can recognise the difference between academic or official industrial sites and personal blogs (web logs) written by non-academics/non-professionals; although it is worth noting that increasingly respected academics are producing their own blogs. Here, it is a case of being familiar with the author's name and status.

One of the ways that you can calculate the reliability of a source is by considering the URL/web address. Often the information contained in the URL can guide you as to whether the web page is of academic use or not. The following acronyms indicate that the information found on these sites is trustworthy:

> **.ac** (academic) college/university UK
> **.edu** (educational institution) outside UK
> **.gov** (government) local and national
> **.org** non-profit organisation
> **.co** company or commercial organisation UK
> **.com** company or commercial organisation any country

The first two indicators (**.ac** and **.edu**) suggest that information on these pages will be the most useful as they are affiliated with educational institutions. Likewise, the **.gov** should contain correct information as these sites are maintained by the government. The last two instances are not as reliable as they are used to promote specific companies and therefore you need to check that information is not biased.

As with all research, the best way to check whether information is reliable is to cross-reference. Cross-referencing on the internet is quick and simple. You can always cut and paste a statement into a key word search in order to investigate whether the same material is available elsewhere. However, be aware that many non-academic sites also use the process of cutting and pasting; as a result you can often find the same incorrect information, word-for-word, on different sites. Once more it is wise to cross-reference key ideas against information located on more reliable sites or in academic books and journals in order to verify their accuracy.

Other reputable and important websites for film scholars include the following:

www.bfi.org.uk (British Film Institute)
www.bufvc.ac.uk (British Universities Film and Video Council)
www.imdb.com (Internet Movie Database)
www.bbc.co.uk (British Broadcasting Corporation)

INTERNET DIRECTORIES

Most universities subscribe to various directories of online academic resources. It is definitely worthwhile to see what such facilities have to offer. The best way of finding these resources is by accessing links from your institution's library page. There are many different directories that you may have access to, but the most renowned are:

- Resource Directory Network (RDN): www.rdn.ac.uk
- BUBL: Film studies: www.bubl.ac.uk
- Info mine: http://infomine.ucr.edu
- Virtual Library: http://vlib.org

Remember these are directories, not individual web pages; therefore be prepared to search for specific topics within the resource. However, using academic directories means that the information returned from your search is typically reliable and of a good academic quality.

71

ATHENS

Athens is a facility used in higher education and further education institutions. It is a system that allows you to log-on to sites that are not necessarily open to the general public. The reason why you may not be permitted access to certain sites is because they require a subscription fee. All universities subscribe to key databases, journals and directories relevant to Film Studies. However, when working from home, on computers that are not networked to the university, you need some way of identifying your affiliation with your home institution. Athens has been developed to enable permission to sites that have been paid for by your university.

Traditionally students had to register in order to gain a username and password to be able to use Athens. More recently, Universities are opting for the 'Alternative Log-in' facility. This means when you try to enter a site that the university has access to, but are working from home and therefore not identified as a student, you can click on the 'Alternative Log-in' option. The traditional Athens log-in is still available on most sites so if you have been allocated a username and password you can choose this option instead. If you choose 'Alternative Log-in' then you are automatically re-routed to one of two pages. Either you will find a long list of institutions – if this is the case then you must identify the name of your university from a long list (if you cannot find your specific university try and think laterally: if Keele University is not on the list, try looking for the University of Keele instead). Conversely you may be relocated to a log-in page that is affiliated with your home university and here you would log-in as normal – using your own university username and password.

ONLINE DIGITALLY SCANNED ARTICLES

One of the best resources available to you as a student is journal articles. Within your department, decisions are made as to which journals will best support your Film Studies programme. Traditionally journals are kept in the library, but more recently when the latest volumes become available the library receives them in two formats: as a hard copy of the magazine/periodical, and as a digitally scanned copy.

The digital version of the journal should be readily available for you to read online. This is typically accessed through an electronic link from the online library catalogue. Alternatively, your university will subscribe to a number of databases that house many different journals from all disciplines. Amongst the best of these databases are the following:

- JSTOR: www.jstor.org
- Film and Television Literature Index with Full Text (Hosted by EBSCO)

Alternatively there are sites that recommend journal articles, yet do not provide links to pdf versions of full articles. One of the main databases that give this information is 'Film Index International', which is run by the BFI (British Film Institute), and therefore it provides great listings for all articles covered in *Sight and Sound*, amongst other publications. The web address for this database is: Film Index International: http://fii.chadwyck.co.uk/home. Bear in mind you can only use this resource if your university has subscribed to it.

WEB JOURNALS

In addition to the traditional Journals that you find in your university library, there are more and more journals being created specifically for the internet. Film Studies is an area where such journals are beginning to emerge. Academic web journals differ greatly from sites set up by fans to discuss the latest Hollywood offerings – so once more it is important that you distinguish between the populist web pages about general film and the scholarly writing available on the net. The following are academic web sites:

- www.sensesofcinema.com
- www.brightlightsfilm.com
- www.kinoeye.org
- www.scope.nottingham.ac.uk
- www.film-philosophy.com

KEEPING UP TO DATE

As the internet is constantly expanding, with new web articles, blogs and reviews appearing by the minute, it is important that you try and keep abreast of new information that is relevant to your studies. One of the ways in which you can do this is by subscribing to an alert system whereby an email will be sent to your email account telling you when new information comes online.

Google alerts enable you to register key words: for example if you are working on a particular director, star, national cinema or period of film-making, they will keep you informed of any new writings on the topic. However, you should be aware that much of the material you receive will come from popular newspaper articles, or people's personal blogs, so much of it will not be useful. Nevertheless, you will find some relevant items of information. Also, be aware that Google alerts can rapidly inundate your in-box, so you need to monitor your account regularly.

Likewise, Amazon will send you email alerts based on your purchasing history; if you have bought a number of books by a particular author, or DVDs by a specific director, they will take previous purchases into account and inform you when similar items appear. Zetoc is another alert service maintained by the British Library. It is more relevant to postgraduate researchers as it notifies its subscribers of up-and-coming conferences; however, it would be useful to you as this service sends content information for journals that may be of interest to your studies. Amazon does not offer a subscription policy, but will send you emails independently based on what you have ordered in the past; however, the other two services mentioned can be found at the following sites:

- www.google.com/alerts
- http://zetoc.mimas.ac.uk

NEWSPAPERS

Traditionally researchers would often visit specialist libraries to view old newspapers and trade papers via microfilm and microfiche. However, much of this material has been transferred to a digital format which you can now view online. Many newspapers have their own homepages which archive old articles, interviews with film-makers, movie reviews etc. . . . for your perusal.

Nexis UK is a facility that your university may subscribe to. This resource houses newspapers, magazines, industry newsletters, trade press, media transcripts, newswires, press releases and over 300 blog sites. These sources are mainly contemporary and updated daily, but do date back to 1975. There are also over 12,000 international news sources for you to consult. If you find an article of particular interest you can send it to your email account.

FINDING FILMS

As a film scholar the fundamental resource for your studies are films themselves. It is important that you use these primary sources in all aspects of your work, whether engaging in textual analysis of your written work or providing illustrations for your presentations. Over the years the way academics have accessed films has changed considerably. When Film Studies was first conceived as an academic discipline, Universities would order film reels for students to

75

watch. This practice was soon replaced with the development of videos and DVDs.

Your department may have a library or resource centre where you can view films or borrow them overnight. Furthermore, it is worth investigating your local public library as they also have films that you can take out. Alternatively you can subscribe to an online rental service where DVDs will be sent to your home. For a relatively small amount of money you will receive 3–4 films per month: such companies include LOVEFiLM.com, Amazon.co.uk, and Sofacinema.co.uk.

If you know a film will be of particular use for an assignment, you may want to consider purchasing your own copy. Most films are available for purchase on the high street or online. If you are having difficulties locating a film then you could try specialist companies, such as moviemail-online.co.uk, that specialise in locating foreign language, cult favourites and lesser-known titles. You could also try looking for second-hand copies of deleted titles on Ebay.com

In addition to all these ways of locating films for your research (and pleasure), the internet is fast becoming a means of downloading films and finding clips. Youtube.com and other sites which house extracts (Screen.org, BBC Media Library, BFI Creative Archive) are a fantastic way of sourcing popular and unusual clips. These extracts can range from avant-garde shorts, early silent moves, hard-to-find foreign language films, etc. . . . The wealth and breadth of film clips is surprising and can really enhance your viewing culture.

VLE: VIRTUAL LEARNING ENVIRONMENT

A VLE is an online space where you will find access to electronic learning materials. In this day and age, more and more universities, and further educational institutions, are encouraging the use of online resources to support the learning needs of students. Webct,

Blackboard and Moodle are the most successful software packages available, but you must investigate what VLE facilities are available for you.

To access your university VLE you will be given a username and password. Once you log on to the site you should then find links to the specific units/modules that you are taking. Each individual unit is typically maintained by a lecturer, and the amount of information you find available will often vary. However, you should find a combination of the following: electronic handbooks/module documents about course content, electronic journal articles, links to useful websites, discussion boards, feedback forms and supplementary information about assessments, and maybe even some online assignments for you to complete. When you are online using your VLE make sure you familiarise yourself with the many functions that are available; for example you can often take notes electronically whilst doing an online reading.

The great thing about a VLE is that you can access the information at a time that suits you. This is really beneficial for students who have part-time jobs; you can read material relevant to your course any time of day or night.

Chapter 10

Viewing skills

Van Norris

PREPARATION FOR DISCUSSION

Think about how you watch films. Is there a difference in the way you watch a set film that you are studying and the way you watch a film at the cinema or at home for fun?

INTRODUCTION

Textual analysis involves making detailed notes of each relevant aspect of film or production that you are studying. This is a process which helps us isolate how a text functions and operates. We thus investigate how a film text works in terms of cinematography and editing, mise-en-scène, sound and music and narrative. This increases our understanding of a given film. Reading a film is part of a process and there is no set formula which can be used to reach a simplistic set of fixed answers. There are no absolutes in this area of study.

It is important to remember that film is a highly complex creative medium. A lot of time and effort is spent putting a film together from pre-production to completion. Always consider when watching a film other ways in which it could have been made, and how else the subject matter could have been approached. Why did the production team make these particular choices? Imagine the endless possibilities and multiple decisions that have been implemented when you watch a film. Another thing to remember is that the more textual work you engage with the more developed your readings will be, and the more confident you will become in peeling away the layers of meaning in a sequence.

Film, as a discipline, bears a lot of similarities with the more traditional academic subject of English Literature. Many of the ways we approach reading films as texts borrow from theoretical approaches used in literary studies, including semiotics, structuralism and post-structuralism. Whereas in English Literature you would be expected to undertake in-depth analysis of a piece of prose, paying close attention to sentence construction and grammar, in Film Studies you are similarly required to deconstruct scenes paying attention to visual cues and editing. In fact, Film Studies can be thought of as sharing approaches with literary analysis as both disciplines attempt to locate texts within their creative, cultural and historical settings.

Furthermore, film shares many parallels with fine art as they are both visual mediums. Many directors rely on the same lighting and compositional rules as painters and will be leaving the same kinds of visual cues in their work. Martin Scorsese, for example, cites the Italian Baroque artist Caravaggio's framing, colour and use of religious symbolism in his films such as *Mean Streets* (1973) and *Goodfellas* (1990). So it is helpful to be aware of this fundamental relationship between canvas and celluloid and to appreciate the medium with the same sense of gravitas as you would a painting.

Denotation and connotation

When you are carrying out textual analysis it is important to remember the two key terms of denotation and connotation. This is a handy way to separate and unpack how we interpret film imagery.

Denote

Denote refers to what you are literally/physically seeing on the screen. Many people rush straight towards what they think the *symbolic* meaning might be without describing what it is they are actually seeing and hearing. How can we begin to analyse symbolic meanings before we are clear about what *exactly* is in the frame?

Connote

Connote is concerned with any association implied by a particular image, with a focus on possible symbolic or abstract messages. By connotation we mean the cultural/social/textual significance of an image (or indeed a piece of dialogue) and how that is represented in this context. For example Dorothy's ruby slippers in the *Wizard of Oz* (Victor Fleming, 1939) could simply be seen as an item of footwear (denote); however, they come to represent home, family and safety (connote).

FOCUSING YOUR TEXTUAL ANALYSIS

The best textual analysis will demonstrate some level of background knowledge. For instance, an understanding of generic conventions, familiarity with other films by the same director, political, social and economic conditions, will all help to contextualise your interpretation of the visual signs. Otherwise, what we will be left with will be merely a set of vague, ungrounded ideas that give a guessed impression of what the intent might be.

This is important as you need to demonstrate a sense of cultural competency in your work. It is not enough to comment on formal elements within the frame without analysing their purpose. You need to interpret these elements, and explain the overall meaning and effect created.

Critically what sets apart a film in terms in perceptions of quality and weight is how directors manipulate formal components. This is simply the individual constituents of the film form itself, such as editing, framing, colour, sound, music, camera movement etc. The perceived quality of a film text will often reside not just in how complex or logical the plot is or how clever the dialogue is, or how convincing the performances of the actors seem to be; 'quality' is often assessed by just *how* a director combines these formal elements.

Ideally, you should engage in textual analysis after you have already seen the film; this will prevent you from focusing on the story. Remember, lecturers do not want a 'surface' set of plot descriptions, but rather an analytical approach. Though you are discussing an *artistic* practice it may help to think of the film as a mechanism that you are taking apart to see exactly how it works. Remember that the director is not responsible for all of the aspects of the film, and make sure you credit the cinematographer or editor, or relevant crew member when discussing specific aspects. This doesn't mean that you have to be a film technician, but knowing some key film-making terminology will undoubtedly add a precision to your written analysis.

Keeping the following categories in mind will help to focus your reading of a film or short sequence. Remember everything in the frame, on the screen and in the dialogue is there for a reason.

Cinematography and Editing

Using terminology such as pans, fades, dissolves, tracking shots, medium, close-ups, head and shoulder shots etc. will bring concision to your visual analysis. See a good film glossary if you're unsure of any of technical film terms (books or internet).

Is the editing significant? Is the editing intrusive? Is it stylised in any way? Is it linear? Are there long 'takes' or are the shots very quickly cut together? Are there noticeably few cuts?

Camera movement can, in many instances, be seen as important. What is being offered as directed viewing? What are we being positioned to look at as an audience by the camera positions (or indeed perhaps been encouraged to look *away* from?).

Does the camera move around a lot? Is it fixed? Are there any angles here that stand out? If so, why and what purpose do they serve?

Is the way the camera is placed telling you something here? 'Canted' or tilted angles, for example, can take on great significance at dramatic or supernatural moments – this is something you will notice in many thrillers or horror films when trying to subliminally impart anxiety or stress.

Sound and Music

Locate the source of the music. Is it part of the narrative world (diegesis), e.g. does it come from a radio, or are the characters singing? If so this is referred to as diegetic. If you cannot identify the source of the music, and it is external to the narrative world, then the term non-diegetic is used. Occasionally filmmakers play with these devices by merging the two forms – in this case it is known as extra-diegetic.

Is the music important in the film text? Film-makers use music as a source of meaning in order to add an additional layer of meaning to the narrative.

Is the *lack* of music important? Remember silence is often the composer's greatest weapon.

Does the scene feature a song or piece of music which adds to the meaning of a scene? Are the lyrics of a song important?

Consider why you think a certain set of sounds or sound effects are employed, highlighted or perhaps even ignored.

Is the sound incongruous or awkward?

Is it noteworthy that certain sounds are placed higher in the 'mix' of a soundtrack?

Does a specific song enhance the meaning of a scene? Are the lyrics of a song played within a scene important?

Consider the orchestration of the music. Which instruments are being used and how does this add to the tone of the sequence?

Mise-en-scène

Keep a note of what happens within the frame. How is the scene composed? Are the characters central, obscured, scattered or combined? Is the framing tight, open with lots of space or is it broken up in any way?

Are there power relationships detectable? Is there a hierarchy observable within the shot?

Is the lighting notable in your clip? Is light employed in a specific way and indeed, is this important? Is the lighting 'bright', is it 'dark', is it specifically angled or could it be described as 'naturalistic' in any way?

What can you notice about the setting and backgrounds, the art design? Does this tell us anything about the characters, their internal 'life', their psychology, the setting, their moral position, the story, their social class, the mood etc?

Acting style too is important and can be considered a formal element. Each character will be portrayed and presented in a very specific fashion for reasons pertinent to the text. Each performance contains another set of precise artistic choices.

Consider the use of dialogue: what expressions are used, what tone do the characters take? Also, make note of specific uses of language and accents.

Costume can be a signifier; clothes offer much information about the 'internal' as well as the 'external' life of a character.

What colours are used within the film? Are they significant? What do they connote? Don't fall into obvious traps of stating prescribed clichés, i.e. 'the suit is red which represents passion or anger'.

Narrative and Plot

Consider the way language is used in the film. What does it tell you about the characters (class distinctions, regional accents, national identities)?

Does the film conform to or subvert any generic conventions (musicals, westerns, sci-fi, horror etc.).

Does the narrative structure follow the classical Hollywood model or is it experimental?

Intertextuality

Does the scene remind you of another scene from a film? If so, how and why? Do you think this in itself might hold meaning?

Some directors, such as Quentin Tarantino, *Kill Bill* 1 (2003) and 2 (2004), or Baz Luhrmann's *Moulin Rouge!* (2000) 'quote' cinema and popular culture in the same way literary writers cite other plays or books.

Occasionally a quotation may be in place because it offers a range of complex signals to the audience, some of which may well be direct, some indirect and some ironic and deliberately humorous.

Draw on your own cultural competency and question why references to other texts (be they musical, literary, artistic or filmic) are being used.

SEMINAR EXERCISE

Watch a short sequence from *Romeo and Juliet* (Baz Luhrmann, 1996) and in groups of 3 or 4 analyse the formal qualities used. Ensure that you consider all of the categories mentioned above and be prepared to discuss your findings with the rest of the class.

Although there may be some obvious answers or observations that may be drawn from looking at a film closely it is also worth bearing in mind that this may often not just be a prescribed formula to reach a simplistic set of fixed answers; i.e. 'the hat is black which means that the man is evil', etc. Meaning will be more complex and nuanced than this. Textual analysis can often be a subjective and sometimes slippery aspect of study. Creative thought in university work is always valued (especially in this area), as long as it is grounded with solid knowledge of the film, informed by context and the creative personnel that you are looking at, and your readings aren't just based on a series of impressionistic, vague assumptions.

Many people outside Film Studies often wrongly assume that reading a film this closely will spoil your enjoyment of film. Not so.

This will deepen your viewing pleasure and will enable you to truly enjoy cinema at all its various complex levels. This is, after all, a visual medium and should be enjoyed as such. It should be that you will begin to enjoy film in a richer, deeper way and see just how clever your favourite filmmakers really are.

FILM SCREENINGS AT UNIVERSITY

As Film Studies students you are required to attend screenings of set films for the majority of your units. It is important to take part in the collective viewing process, which allows you to watch the film on a big screen without interruptions. Even if you have seen the film previously and own it on DVD, it is still wise to attend the screenings to refresh your memory and to have an opportunity to experience with others the excitement, fear, disgust and any other emotions that come your way.

TIPS FOR FILM SCREENINGS

- Make sure you are active in the viewing process.
- Be prepared; always have a pen and something to write on.
- Try not to take eyes from screen when writing as you may miss something important.
- It is not easy to write in the dark, but don't let this deter you from making brief notes and reminders of the film.
- Don't worry about the coherence and legibility of your notes as you are the only person who will have to read them.
- Try writing in large block letters and use several pages of paper
- Pen lights are available to buy from the internet and they can help dramatically with your note-taking.

You are expected to respect other students in the screening, therefore, do not talk throughout the film as this is highly distracting. Remember film screenings are an academic exercise.

FURTHER READING

Bordwell, D. and Thompson. K. *Film Art: An Introduction*. New York: McGraw-Hill, 1993.

Cook, P. (ed.). *The Cinema Book*. London: BFI, 2000.

Monaco, J. *How to Read a Film*. Oxford: OUP, 1981.

Nelmes, J. *Introduction to Film Studies*. London: Routledge, 1996.

Chapter 11

How to watch and study foreign language films

Réka Buckley and Deborah Shaw

PREPARATION

In groups, note down all the foreign language movies that you have seen in the past year, and comment on your experience of watching them.

INTRODUCTION

As students on a Film Studies degree programme you will inevitably be required to watch numerous foreign language films throughout your time at university. As film students and film enthusiasts you will no doubt have already watched many films in a range of languages. You may have studied some of the classics of French New Wave, German Expressionism and Italian Neorealist cinema during your college courses. You may also be familiar with a range of national cinemas such as the contemporary cult scene emerging from East Asia, recent Bollywood movies and films from Latin America. Whatever your experience, this chapter will give you some useful tips on how to prepare for studying foreign language films. It will introduce you to some of the problems that you might face and propose some solutions. Finally, this chapter will offer you guidance on how to get the most out of the foreign language films

89

that you watch. We are assuming that the implied reader of this section is a native English speaker, although, of course, this may not be the case.

SEMINAR EXERCISE

In a group consider and discuss the following:

1 Why is it important to study foreign language films on a Film Studies degree?
2 What can you gain from studying foreign language films?
3 Are you in favour or against the idea of multiplex cinemas showing more foreign language films?
4 Why are some people resistant to watching subtitled films?

RESISTANCE TO WATCHING FOREIGN LANGUAGE FILMS

Many people are resistant to watching foreign language films. At a recent screening of the film *The Orphanage/El orfanato* (Juan Antonio Bayona, 2007), the person selling the tickets was warning the customers that this was a foreign film. He explained when asked why he felt the need to do this that many people had walked out and complained when they realised that the film was in Spanish. Why should this be the case, and why are so many people resistant to watching films in another language and with subtitles? This question is impossible to answer without carrying out detailed audience-focused research; however, it probably has to do with a desire for familiarity, and the sense that reading subtitles is hard work. In addition, in contrast to globally oriented Hollywood films, distributors do not inject the same amount of funds into marketing campaigns, so audiences may remain unaware of the precise nature of these films or their subject matter.

Nevertheless, much can be gained from watching films from a range of national contexts. This includes the opportunity to appreciate different forms of storytelling to dominant Hollywood models; the chance to gain an insight into other cultures and languages; the pleasure from learning about other national cinemas; and finally, the chance to watch some excellent films that you would otherwise miss. It would be a great shame to have missed the following films (to name but a few), simply because of a professed aversion to subtitles: *Battle Royale* (Fukasaku, 2001), *City of God* (Meirelles, Lund, 2002), *Downfall* (Hierschbiegel, 2004), *House of Flying Daggers* (Yimou Zhang, 2004), *The Motorcycle Diaries* (Salles, 2004), *Hidden/Caché* (Haneke, 2005), *The Lives of Others* (Henckel von Donnersmarck, 2006), *Volver* (Almodóvar, 2006). With a good film that really holds your attention, you will find that you are not even aware that you are reading subtitles and that the film is not in English.

PREPARATION FOR WATCHING FOREIGN LANGUAGE FILMS FOR STUDY

The more prepared you are, the more enjoyment and understanding you can gain from watching a foreign language film.

Foreign language films are usually set and filmed in a different socio-cultural context to your own, so it is always helpful to your overall understanding and appreciation of the text to come to screenings with a bit of background information or knowledge of the film you are about to watch.

- Look at the reading list in your course handbook and identify which texts are relevant to the film that you are about to watch.
- Find out information about the film's director/stars etc. For example, if you are expected to watch *The Discreet Charm of the Bourgeoisie* (1972), then information gathered on the director

Luis Buñuel, such as his social, cultural, religious and political outlook, will prove essential in helping you to understand the content and themes covered in his film.

■ When studying a foreign language film it's essential to have some knowledge of the socio-cultural and political environment in which the film was made and set. If you watch the Italian Neorealist film *Rome Open City* (Roberto Rossellini, 1945), then it would greatly aid your understanding of the film if you were aware of key historical facts.

■ It is very easy when watching a foreign language film to concentrate your attention on the subtitles and not focus on the images. Try to make sure that you pay as much attention to the images as to the subtitles.

PROBLEMS YOU MIGHT ENCOUNTER WITH DUBBED AND SUBTITLED FILMS:

Subtitled films

■ You may miss some of the images as you are engaged with reading the subtitles. Watching and listening are different skills to reading, and occur at a different pace. For this reason, subtitlers have to leave out some of the original words and summarise the content of the language to fit into the frame.

■ Subtitles do not always accurately capture the original language; thus, in certain instances they may not correctly translate the dialogue.

■ Puns and specific cultural references may be lost in translation. The quality of the translation is also not always particularly good. The calibre and competence of the translator is important in translating not only the words but also the meanings and nuances of the original language.

■ The text is often written in white and at times the scenery is light in colour so there is little contrast between the two. As a result of this, it can be difficult to read the subtitles.

Dubbed films

Dubbing is typically used for Hollywood films that are exported around the world, and is less commonly used with 'world cinema' film texts. As with subtitling, there are a number of problematic areas that need to be mentioned here.

■ The voices used to dub the actors might be very different or even inappropriate. The choice of which type of English (American, British, Australian etc.) or which accent (the Queen's English, or a broad Yorkshire accent) can greatly impact on your interpretation of and insight into a particular character.

■ Dubbed films, as with subtitled films, can suffer from the problems of linguistic and cultural nuances which can be lost in the cultural transfer of the language.

■ Audiences can feel disconnected from the characters emotionally, and be dissatisfied with not being able to hear the original voices.

STUDYING FOREIGN LANGUAGE FILMS

There are a number of ways of overcoming problems associated with watching subtitled films, particularly those that you are studying on your degree programme. To gain the most from a film (particularly those that are not in English), you should be prepared to watch it several times. First watch the film the whole way through without pausing. This way you gain an overall understanding of the storyline and characters. Then watch it again in your own time. Now that you are familiar with the plot you will be able to pay more attention to the images. By being able to pause the film, you will also be able to follow the dialogue as well as the action in a more satisfactory manner. The more subtitled films that you watch, the easier you will find it.

After you have watched the film, it is a good idea to make notes regarding central themes, forms of representation, the use of cinematic techniques etc. . . . ., as this will help you when revising for your end-of-semester tests or for preparing your essays.

SEMINAR EXERCISE

Watch a scene from a subtitled film twice. First time watch the clip with the subtitles, second time cover them up. Be prepared to comment on the difference in the viewing experience. What did you gain and lose in the second viewing?

Foreign language films often struggle to make their presence felt at the box office for a number of reasons, many of which are discussed above. However, they are central to Film Studies students' cinematic knowledge. You cannot claim to have a background in the discipline if you are unfamiliar with films by Bergman, Godard, Renoir, Eistenstein, Lang, Buñuel, Fellini, Kurosawa, Almodóvar, von Trier, Kieslowski, Tarkovsky and Satyajit Ray, to name but a few directors.

Chapter 12

Essay writing

Christine Etherington-Wright

INTRODUCTION

Many students find essay writing challenging. The aim of this chapter is to divide this process into 'bite-size' stages, which will enable you to achieve a clear and persuasive academic writing style. To make your meaning clear you need to work out exactly what you are going to say about a topic and communicate this in a confident and logical manner. All students can improve with practice and attention to detail.

> **SEMINAR EXERCISE**
>
> What do you think are the differences between essay writing at 'A' level and as an undergraduate?
> What makes a good essay? Write down your ideas.

THINGS TO DO BEFORE YOU START WRITING

- Read *all* the essay questions carefully before you select one. Take your time: this is a very important stage.
- Remember, to achieve a good mark you must be able to address all parts of the question.

- <u>Underline</u> or **highlight** key words in the question, (this will ensure that you read carefully and do not miss out vital information).
- Note how long your essay should be.

HOW DO YOU START TO FORM YOUR ANSWER?

Mindmaps are a good way of developing and structuring your ideas. These can take many forms (spider diagram, flow chart, grid, etc.). We have included a spider diagram for the following question:

'Present an analysis of your favourite director, referring to at least three films. Make sure you consider recurring themes, stylistic traits and cultural context.'

The purpose of the spider diagram, or other forms of mindmaps, is to help you process and organise your initial ideas. Remember that this is simply a starting point. Once you have researched your topic in greater detail you will be able to focus on key areas, as it would be impossible to include so much material in one essay.

SEMINAR EXERCISE

Produce a spider diagram/mind map in preparation for your essay. You must choose a director (not Spike Lee), but remember this is only a preliminary exercise as you will need to carry out research in order to do this properly.

Cultural context

* Race
* Politics
* Music
* Oppression
* Community
* African American
  traditions

Themes

* Race
* Family
* Community
* Poverty/inequality
* Sport
* Gender

SPIKE LEE

Stylistic Traits

* Direct address
* Canted framing
* Extreme camera
  angles
* Dolly shot (actor
  appears to float)
* Music
* Colour

Key film texts

* *Do the Right Thing*
* *Malcolm X*
* *He Got Game*
* *The Inside Man*
* *25th Hour*
* *She's Gotta Have It*
* *Bamboozled*
* *Get on the Bus*

RESEARCH

To write a good essay you need to read. You need to read books and articles; internet sources alone are insufficient (unless you are using electronic academic sources). You need to allow plenty of time to do this. Make sure you note fully the sources you intend to use.

Have the essay title in front of you when you make notes as you need to keep your focus on the essay title. As you are reading, keep the following questions in mind:

How will I use this information?
Is this information important to my argument?

ORGANISATION AND STRUCTURE

An essay needs to be structured. Your essay should take your reader along a carefully planned route. Your route must include all your main points and yet maintain an overall sense of direction. This involves two elements; organising the points you want to make into groups and giving each of these groups a paragraph. The paragraphs then need to be arranged into a meaningful sequence which takes the reader to your conclusion.

The first thing to do is make a plan. This is crucial, as this will help you develop a coherent argument. (An argument is a series of points presented in a logical order, with links from one point to the next.) You need to prioritise the main points of your argument and discard information that is not relevant to the question. Good researchers often have to leave material out as there is simply too much to include. You need to re-work and revise the order of main points until you are sure that you have a logical and effective arrangement in order to begin writing.

Essays require an introductory paragraph, a series of linked paragraphs for the main body of the essay, and a concluding paragraph. These elements combine to form the scaffolding that firmly holds the shape of your essay.

Students up to and including 'A' level standard are often told that an 'introduction' should say what you are going to write about, you then do it in the main body of the essay, and then say what you have done in the 'conclusion'. In essence this is true, but it can be formulaic; tedious to do and read.

Introduction (first paragraph)

You need to work out your argument/discussion before you write this first paragraph. Therefore introductions frequently are written last. Introductions can often be inadequate and often contain irrelevances such as regurgitating/paraphrasing the question.

Begin with a firmly stated idea of what you intend to argue followed by a brief explanation of your method to present this. The introductory paragraph may be a good place to define key terms used in your essay.

Aim for an interesting first sentence to catch your readers' attention. Avoid the dull; 'In this essay I am going to do this, then this, then this . . . ' which reads like a shopping list.

One example of a good way to write an introduction to the question:

'Discuss masculinity in *Robin Hood: Prince of Thieves*'

would be:

'This essay will concentrate on the roles of Robin Hood, Friar Tuck and the Sheriff of Nottingham in order to analyse masculinity in Kevin Reynolds's film. This discussion is divided into three parts, each of which focuses upon a different facet of masculinity. The male hero in classical Hollywood cinema will be the starting point, followed by the masculine body as spectacle, which leads to the final point of masculinity in crisis. These theoretical positions need to be briefly outlined,

99

before being fully explored below, in order that a meaningful discussion may be undertaken.'

The main body

In the paragraphs that make up the main section you need to expand the themes/points identified in the introduction. You are taking your reader through an argument. Work logically and build your argument point by point. Each point needs to be explained, developed and supported in a paragraph of its own.

To do this you need to develop your use of **link** words and **direct the reader** in order that he/she can follow your train of thought. Link words help your essay to flow and to carry the meaning forward from sentence to sentence, paragraph to paragraph.

- They can suggest a change of direction: 'But, However, Conversely, Although, Yet, Subsequently'.
- They can indicate that you are going to add something similar to what has gone before: 'Furthermore, Moreover, Additionally, In addition, Also, As well as'.
- They can show that you are going to conclude an argument and punctuate its significance, e.g. Conversely: 'So, Therefore, Overall'.

At times you also need to indicate, on a broader front, the flow of your discussion. These phrases are useful reminders to the reader from time to time of the argument's direction. Phrases such as: 'It seems that if this is the case . . . ', 'Having discussed . . . it is necessary to look at . . . ', 'As well as . . . , . . . needs to be considered', 'It is now useful to deal with the issue of . . . ', 'The next important use of . . . ', 'In point of fact . . . '.

One final point in this section: you do not have to direct the reader on everything you do. It can become boring and overdone.

Conclusion

In the concluding paragraph you need to give a direct answer to the essay question. There should be a sense of having reached the end. Ask yourself, 'If this paragraph occurred at the bottom of a page would you turn the page expecting more to follow?' If the answer is 'yes' then your conclusion needs to be firmer.

Avoid simple summarising; this is likely to be repetitive and reductive, similar to the 'shopping list' in introductions. It is unlikely to do justice to your essay. Be assertive.

Show how your main points lead to your conclusion(s).

Remember: Do not raise new or unrelated issues in this last paragraph.

Signposting here may include: 'It can be seen from the above that . . . ', 'It has been established that . . . ', 'The earlier points raised lead to the conclusion that . . . ', 'To conclude, throughout this essay it has become apparent that . . . '.

PARAGRAPHS

You need to present your ideas clearly and will need to use paragraphs correctly. Paragraphs are groups of sentences on the same theme.

Successful paragraphs

Successful essays require clearly structured paragraphs

- Each paragraph needs to be centred on a particular issue linked to the question. It should have at least 8–10 lines to establish and develop an idea.
- Each paragraph needs to serve a purpose. Make sure the subject of the paragraph is clear.

- Each paragraph needs to have a connection to what has gone before and what is to follow. Avoid a series of unconnected points.

- You need phrases and words that link points to develop the logical progress to a coherent argument that directly answers the question.

- Is this paragraph relevant to the title? Does this paragraph progress my argument? What is this paragraph adding to my discussion?

TONE, STYLE AND VOICE

In any writing it is important to have a 'sense of reader/audience'. Who should you assume is the reader when you write an essay? Although your tutor reads your essay, he or she is not your 'readership'. The usual advice is to write for an intelligent person who has an interest in your topic and would like to know more. Try to avoid unnecessary information that is not relevant to the question, for example in-depth biographical details.

It is *very* important to write in sentences. If you are unsure if you have written a sentence ask yourself 'Does it have a subject and a verb?' If you find this is not obvious to you, you will need to get some help with grammar. Otherwise, you will find it difficult to develop your own style to express yourself and you will lose marks.

It takes time to find a writing 'voice'. In academic writing you should present yourself as a calm detached observer; unbiased, pointing out some arguments that are relevant to the question ('for heavens sake!' avoid emotive expression and exclamation marks). This is one of the main reasons that starting your essay can be difficult as you are trying to work out where you are 'coming from'.

In academic writing it is traditionally considered inappropriate to use the first person, 'I/We'. It is more acceptable to use the third person, 'He/She/It'. This is straightforward when referring to other people's work, but it is not so easy when giving your view. How is this done?

Give your opinions indirectly using the passive voice. For example: 'I think that . . . ' can become, 'It could be thought that . . . '. Above all avoid 'I feel . . . '. Academic writing is not about your feelings; it is concerned with reflective, balanced argument based on evidence.

QUOTATIONS AND SOURCES

Use a good range of sources and comment on them. Use more than one source for a whole section of your essay. Quotations must be introduced, contextualised and commented upon.

> Poor use of quotation: *Dead Man* is a character-driven narrative, in this film, 'Plot is stripped away in Jarmusch's films, with events emerging from distinctive personality traits of the characters and the nature of their interactions' (Nelmes, 2003, p. 147).
>
> Good use of quotation: *Dead Man* is a character-driven narrative; Nelmes argues that, 'Plot is stripped away in Jarmusch's films, with events emerging from distinctive personality traits of the characters and the nature of their interactions' (2003, p. 147). This can be seen when . . . etc.

Do not use too many quotes. We want to know your opinions and ideas. Remember, an essay is not a collage of academic citations! Also, it is not necessary to quote every time that you take a point from a critical source. You can put the writer's views in your own words and still cite the source. Only use quotations when the critic says something that is impressively written or memorable.

An unnecessary quote: Jarmusch's films are characterised by 'a really interesting use of narrative techniques' (Allen, 2002, p. 302).

A good use of quotation would be:

In her discussion of episodic structure in film, Nelmes argues that:

> this character-centred approach to film-making also permeates the structure of Jarmusch's films. Instead of a coherent narrative strain, the films proceed thematically through their own internal thematic logic (2003, p. 147).

Always present quotations correctly. Look closely at the above quotations. In the case of quotations that are shorter than three lines in length, use quotation marks and place within the body of the paragraph. Quotations that are three lines or more should be indented. Also leave a line before and after the quotation and omit quotation marks here.

VOCABULARY FOR ESSAY WRITING

To help develop a more academic tone or academic language you may find some of the following verbs useful.

To Describe: define, identify, outline, select, present, recognise, repeat, state

To Comprehend/ Understand: interpret, comprehend, clarify, defend, distinguish, explain, generalise, exemplify, give examples of, infer, summarise, discuss, present, illustrate, indicate, select, understand, contrast, compare, demonstrate, change, show, find, assess

To Analyse: recognise, distinguish, evaluate, differentiate, identify, infer, outline, point out, compare, contrast, justify, devote, conclude, criticise

To Synthesise: Propose, present, structure, develop, create, devise, explain, generate, summarise, report, argue, put together, suggest

To Evaluate: judge, appraise, assess, conclude, compare, contrast, juxtapose, describe how, criticise, justify, defend, evaluate, determine, question

COMMON MISTAKES

Spell checker

It is important to remember that the spell checker will not pick up all mistakes.

- 'typos', e.g. 'form' where you intended to write 'from'
- The spell checker does not know the grammatical sense of the word; for example, 'there' instead of 'their'

Common spelling mistakes

- definate – should be 'definite' (think of 'finite')
- independant – should be 'independent'
- loose (as in loose a cricket match) – should be 'lose a cricket match'
- who's and whose
- principal – the main figure, the head of a school
- principle – a fundamental truth, a moral principle
- stationery – writing paper
- stationary – not moving, immobile
- practice – the noun, 'Doctor's practice'
- practise – the verb, 'students need to practise essay writing'
- affect = a verb; effect = a noun – e.g. 'the special effects affect the way that the film was received'
- Don't forget the 'i' before 'e' except after 'c' rule – as in 'believe' but 'receive'

Apostrophes

This is an area where many students have difficulty and make mistakes. Incorrect use can either change the meaning of a sentence or make it meaningless.

The apostrophe is used to denote possession. If there is one 'owner' the apostrophe is placed before the 's':

> **Hitchcock's** films, **Britain's** film industry (there is one Hitchcock and one Britain).

If there is more than one 'owner' the apostrophe is placed after the 's':

> The **actor's** relationship with the director – only one actor
> The **actors'** relationship with the director – more than one actor

Remember the following:

> it's = it is
> its = its (possessive)
> It's a good film; its main qualities can be seen in the use of cinematography.

From this example you can see that the apostrophe is used to show that a letter has been omitted (it's), therefore it is important to remember this when writing 'don't' (do not), 'shouldn't' (should not) and so on. It therefore follows that when writing 1950s, 1960s, 1990s then is **no** apostrophe. **Nothing** has been omitted in these dates.

TIPS AND ADVICE

- Keep to the word limit. Most institutions will penalise you if your essay is 10 per cent over or under the limit.
- Always include a word count at the end of your essay.
- Your essay should not just express an opinion or feelings. It must advance an argument.
- Aim for depth not breadth. In other words, don't just produce a list of points; it is better to have fewer points and fully develop them.
- The basis of all good writing is clarity. Clarity arises from clear thought and simplicity of style. Aim to be clear, precise and concise.
- Use short sentences and straightforward syntax; your prose will sound less clumsy.
- Remember, use italics for all film and book titles.
- Assume that the reader has not read and viewed what you have but that they are interested in the topic offered in the title.
- Avoid personalised statements, for example, 'I feel', 'I believe', 'In my view'.
- Avoid 'we', 'you', use instead 'the audience', 'the reader'.
- Avoid clichés like the plague.
- Avoid overusing brackets (however useful they appear) as they are (for the most part) unnecessary.
- Pay attention to grammar and spelling at all times. Many marks are lost due to poor writing.
- Before handing the work in always proofread your work. Reading aloud is a good way to find errors.

BIBLIOGRAPHY

Nelmes, J. (2003), *An Introduction to Film Studies. 3rd Edition*. London and New York: Routledge.

Chapter 13

Referencing and plagiarism

Lincoln Geraghty

Why academics reference the work they use to write essays, books and articles comes down to two important reasons, academic honesty and good research skills. The first is crucial, and forms the bedrock of academic publishing. We reference the work we quote from or use to further our own arguments so that we can properly acknowledge where we found the source and who said the things we are quoting. It is simply the honest thing to do. If we fail to acknowledge where we get ideas and words from that are not our own then that is called plagiarism and it is an offence in any higher education institution. If we try to reference work we use, but poorly (perhaps not giving exact page numbers), then that is called poor scholarship and is also something that as a student you must learn to avoid. The second reason for referencing is that it shows that you have done research when writing or preparing for your essay. From the work you quote from and the bibliography at the end of your essay, the reader can see how you have researched the topic; they can see the books you have read, and, if they so wish, they can then use your references as a stepping stone for their own research. Both reasons for referencing signal the fact that as an undergraduate you are entering the world of academia and scholarship, where ideas and arguments are offered, shared and contested regularly. Being part of that world as a student means you have to become familiar with both the academic field you are studying and the rules and formats of referencing that the field uses when publishing research.

LEARNING TO REFERENCE PROPERLY

There are several systems of referencing that are used in academic work; you will be told by your tutors which one you need to use in your essays. The three main examples which are outlined in this chapter are **Harvard APA** (APA stands for American Psychological Association), **MLA** (Modern Language Association) and **Chicago**.

Part of the problem attached to student approaches to essay writing is that you can feel isolated from the academic discipline when you first arrive at university. Making the leap from A-Level to degree level can be hard, especially if you are unfamiliar with the methods and traditions of higher education teaching practices, such as the lecture and seminar, or the types of assessment such as the extended critical essay. You are expected to read widely and be critical of the texts you consume. Perhaps try and remember that you are at the beginning of your studies and "are undertaking" what D'Andrea and Gosling call "a 'cognitive apprenticeship'", where you "are metaphorically moving from the 'periphery' of a subject to becoming proficient in it" (D'Andrea and Gosling, 2005, pp. 86–87).

Students today feel anxious about what they must do, learn and complete when they first embark on their degree course, so it is imperative that you are aware of the expectations that tutors have. Referencing in particular can be a huge stumbling block for students unfamiliar with the discipline of essay writing; it can be seen by some as an "elaborate code" which may seem useless and unimportant (D'Andrea and Gosling, 2005, p. 90). However, it must be mastered to attain the higher marks you quite rightly want to achieve. When using references in your essays you must remember that you are participating in an academic discourse, an exchange of knowledge, between yourself, the reader and the sources you have used when doing your research: "[The] ability to use ideas from sources and referencing [is] essential to the construction of knowledge in the university" (Hendricks and Quinn, 2000, p. 448). Citing sources correctly is your way of communicating the depth of knowledge and breadth of research you have invested in your essay. Students should at the earliest stage realise they are "apprentice" scholars of their disciplines, therefore their work must reflect their expertise. Hendricks and Quinn argue that the errors in referencing some students make in their essays are not surface problems but rather are "connected to a deeper understanding of multi-voiced texts and the construction of knowledge" (Hendricks and Quinn, 2000, p. 456). This should help students appreciate the complexities of undergraduate study and how much reading and research every student has to do to achieve the better grades.

FINDING A VOICE

Over the course of your three years at university you will no doubt encounter a broad range of methods that are used to write essays. Some students base their essays on quite a narrow range of work (often web-based) which is clearly not enough to achieve a high quality mark. Some students seemingly do a lot of research; they have a large bibliography, but often fail to engage with the texts critically. Others appear to go into a lot of critical detail with only a few limited sources, and some manage to find the right balance. What lies at the heart of this variety of student attitudes to writing and researching their assignment is the notion of academic literacy. To achieve academic literacy you will need to learn to develop your own voice that both expresses your views and conforms to certain academic standards inherent within the subject area.

Hanne Bock acknowledges that students' understanding of academic texts is reliant on two factors – contextual knowledge and language competence – "without the former, reading becomes

111

simplistic and subjective; without the latter it becomes associative rather than analytical" (Bock, 1988, p. 25). When researching your assignment it is important to keep in mind that if you concentrate on improving and expanding your language skills as well as your research skills, your understanding of the subject will be heightened and your work will become more analytical. In simple terms, read widely, often, and always keep in mind the academic contexts of the field of study in which the book or article you are reading has been written. Making sure that you find your own voice in an academic essay is also vitally important; it is after all your own work and how you identify yourself within it is an essential skill that can be taken on into your future career path. In a sense, finding your own voice in an academic discussion moves you beyond a surface approach to your learning and assessment.

In combination with developing your own language skills and establishing a critical voice, it is important to emphasise the basic skills of essay writing. How do you paraphrase, take ideas from key texts and use them to enhance your argument, to what extent do you quote or cite your chosen text? A significant number of students do not correctly quote or reference books used when writing essays, suggesting that they are unable to distinguish between the author's own voice (or opinion) and the written text (see Uemlianin, 2000). How you then relate your own work to the work of others you have read is crucial if you are to succeed in familiarising yourself with the subject and expressing yourself within an academic environment (see Mann, 2000).

The predominant form of student assessment in Film Studies, the essay, allows you the chance to create and defend your own argument through critical analysis and concentrated research. University lecturers should not be seen as people who tell students what to write or what to think but, as Philip Martin recognises, as people who encourage "their students to think for themselves, and to understand this process as something operating within a broad academic rationale" (Martin, 2003, p. 304).

112

CITING SOURCES

As has been discussed, using a good range of sources and being able to comment on them in an analytical manner is crucial to the execution of high-quality undergraduate work. Remember:

- Use more than one source for a whole section of your essay.
- Introduce your quotations, comment on them, and don't be afraid to disagree with critics.
- If you agree with critics give your reasons.
- When information is common knowledge (i.e. a director's date and place of birth), you do not need to cite any sources.
- Do not over-use quotations as your own voice can be lost.
- Make sure that every quotation used serves a purpose.

PARAPHRASING

Paraphrasing is where you put the ideas or words of another person or source into your own words, thus not directly quoting them but still communicating the ethos or meaning of the original. It is often more detailed than a simple summary and should still be accompanied by an in-text reference to show the original author's details so that the reader can find the original if they so wish. Paraphrasing is an important academic skill and should be one that informs your essay writing and research. The following example highlights some good practice. The in-text citations used are in Harvard APA format and include author name, publication date and page numbers so that the reader can instantly recognise your reference to the original source. This information is different to the information provided in a bibliography since you are specifically noting page numbers to accurately reference where in the book or article you found the information. Examples of the way in which you use references with paraphrased material in contrast with directly quoted material can be found below.

113

This is a sentence written in an essay with quoted words from Sandvoss's *Fans: The Mirror of Consumption* (2005):

> Taking a multifaceted approach to his study, including sociology and psychoanalysis, Sandvoss seeks to understand both the "interaction between fans" and "the interaction between fans and their object of fandom" (2005, p. 10).

Here is an example where the above material has been paraphrased without a direct quote:

> Studies of fandom can concentrate on both the relationship between fans and the text itself (Sandvoss, 2005, p. 10).

Often students will want to use a longer quotation to highlight the work they have read or the argument of another author they want to discuss. Longer quotes, over 30–40 words in length (or three sentences), should be indented in the essay to mark them out as different to the overall text. They do not have quotation marks and are kept in single-spaced format, as compared to the double spacing of the rest of your work.

Here is an example of an essay with a longer quote inserted (indented) with an in-text citation:

> Therefore, fan communities should no longer be viewed as active resisters of textual meaning (in the guise of "textual poachers" to use Jenkins's term [1992]) but as groups of people whose differing interpretations of the text are influenced by their personal experiences and identity. As Sandvoss says:
>
> > The centre of gravity of social signification has shifted from objectively identifiable textual structures associated with particular class positions to subjectively constituted readings and appropriations of fan texts which also reflect . . .

114

distribution of power . . . between class, gender, age and ethnicity (2005, p. 42).

The above quote from Sandvoss suggests that he is putting forward a new method for fan studies that . . .

Paraphrasing without citing the original text is **poor scholarship,** as the example below demonstrates:

Taking a multifaceted approach to his study, including sociology and psychoanalysis, Sandvoss seeks to understand both the interaction between fans and the interaction between fans and their object of fandom.

Quoting as if it were your own is **plagiarism**:

Taking a multifaceted approach, including sociology and psychoanalysis, this essay seeks to understand both the interaction between fans and the interaction between fans and their object of fandom.

It is necessary to emphasise the importance of referencing within the wider contexts of finding your own critical voice in an essay. Referencing, and becoming familiar with the rules and regulations of Harvard APA, MLA or Chicago is not a tick-box skill that university students should do and pass over, but rather a way of expressing knowledge and expertise of your chosen academic subject.

REFERENCING: THE BASICS

The following examples should be used to help guide and introduce you to the most important forms of referencing you will encounter. It is inevitable that you will need to use a whole range of sources in your essays and the few selected examples will in no way stand as a comprehensive list. Therefore, it is advisable that you visit relevant web pages that explain the specific referencing style used by your department. Furthermore, consult style guidelines published by the relevant association you are using: the guidelines for the three formats discussed in this chapter are cited in the bibliography.

This section will provide illustrative examples of correct referencing adhering to the conventions of Harvard APA, MLA and Chicago. It is important to remember that Harvard APA and MLA formats include in-text forms of citation, i.e. the bibliography (in alphabetical order) contains all names, dates and publication information, while the corresponding in-text citation for the Harvard APA system (as already shown in this chapter) contains name, date and page numbers in parentheses. MLA requires just name and page numbers to be included in the text.

There are two styles of referencing which are both referred to as Chicago and this can cause some confusion. There is the Chicago Manual style of referencing and there is also a referencing system known as Chicago Style or Turabian. The Chicago Manual developed from the guidance given to authors by the University of Chicago Press, whereas Chicago Style was developed by Kate Turabian, who was the dissertation secretary at the University of Chicago, and this system deviates slightly from the Manual style but is ultimately a more condensed version. Both Chicago formats allow you to select either footnotes/endnotes or in-text citations, so if you are asked to use either system of referencing it is a good idea to find out whether your department requires you to use footnotes, endnotes or in-text citations. The differences between Chicago Manual and Turabian are minimal and relate to the capitalisation of titles, dates, punctuation and the placement of citations in the text.

Below are examples for each style of referencing discussed in this chapter; however, the Chicago examples comply with the Manual style.

Single authored books

Type of reference	Harvard APA
In-text	(Altman, 1999, p. 22)
	(Surname, year, page. number/s)
How it should look in the bibliography	Altman, R. (1999). *Film/Genre*. London: BFI Publishing.
	Surname, Initial. (Year). *Title in italics*. Place of publication: Publisher.

Type of reference	MLA
In-text	(Altman 22)
	(Surname page number/s)
Bibliography	Altman, Rick. Film/Genre. London: BFI, 1999.
	Surname, First name. *Title in italics* or underlined. Place: Publisher, year.

Type of reference	Chicago Manual
In-text	(Altman 1999, 22)
	(Surname year, page number/s)
Footnote/Endnote	1. Rick Altman, *Film/Genre*. (London: BFI Publishing, 1999). 22.
	1. Full name, *Title in italics* or underlined. (Place: Publisher, year). Page.
Bibliography	Altman, Rick. *Film/Genre*. London: BFI Publishing, Year.
	Surname, First name. *Title in italics* or underlined. Place: Publisher, year.

Note: MLA and Chicago allow either italics or underlining to indicate titles of book, journals films etc. . . . Most computers have the facility for italics, but be aware that when you use certain fonts the difference between italicized letters and non-italicized letters is very difficult to distinguish. When this is the case the best option is to underline titles. Check which is the preferred format required at your university.

Multi-authored books

Type of reference	Harvard APA
In-text	(Harper & Porter, 2003, pp. 23–24)
	(Surname 1 & Surname 2, year, pp. number/s)
How it should look in the bibliography	Harper, S., & Porter, V. (2003). *British Cinema of the 1950s: The Decline of Deference*. Oxford: Oxford University Press.
	Surname 1, Initial 1, & Surname 2, Initial 2. (year). *Title in italics*. Place: Publisher.

Type of reference	MLA
In-text	(Harper and Porter 23–24)
	(Surname 1 & Surname 2 page number/s)
Bibliography	Harper, Sue, and Vincent Porter. <u>British Cinema of the 1950s: The Decline of Deference</u>. Oxford: Oxford University Press, 2003.
	Surname 1, First name 1, and First name 2 Surname *2. Title in italics* or <u>underlined</u>. Place: Publisher, year.

Type of reference	Chicago Manual
In-text	(Harper and Porter 2003, 23–24)
	(Surname 1 and Surname 2 year, page number/s)
Footnote/Endnote	10. Sue Harper and Vincent Porter, <u>British Cinema of the 1950s: The Decline of Deference</u> (Oxford: Oxford University Press, 2003), 23–24.
	10. First name 1 Surname 1 and First name 2 Surname 2, *Title in italics* or <u>underlined</u>. (Place: Publisher, year), page number/s.
Bibliography	Harper, Sue, and Vincent Porter. *British Cinema of the 1950s: The Decline of Deference*. Oxford: Oxford University Press. 2003.
	Surname 1, First name 1, and First name 2 Surname 2. *Title in italics* or <u>underlined</u>. Place: Publisher, year.

Note: in the Harvard APA example you will see the use of 'pp.'. This indicates that the reference is not contained on one page of the book, but goes onto the following page. If you are using Chicago and referring to a book with multiple authors then note the difference in the order of surname and first names depending on whether you are referencing in the bibliography or including details in a footnote/endnote.

Edited books

Type of reference	Harvard APA
In-text	(Kapell & Lawrence, 2006, p. 48)
	(Surname 1 & Surname 2, year, page. number/s)
How it should look in the bibliography	Kapell, M. W., & Lawrence, J. S. (Eds.). (2006). *Finding the Force of the Star Wars Franchise: Fans, Merchandise and Critics*. New York: Peter Lang.
	Editor 1, Initial 1, & Editor 2, Initial 2 (Eds.). (Year). *Title in italics*. Place: Publisher.

Type of reference	MLA
In-text	(Lawrence 2006, 133)
	(Surname year, page number/s)
Bibliography	Kapell, Matthew Wilhelm, and John Shelton Lawrence, eds. <u>Finding the Force of the Star Wars Franchise: Fans, Merchandise and Critics</u>. New York: Peter Lang, 2006.
	Ed 1 Surname, Ed 1 First name/s, and Ed 2 First name/s Ed 2 Surnames, eds. *Title in italics* or <u>underlined</u>. Place: Publisher, year.

Type of reference	Chicago Manual
In-text	(Lawrence 2006, 133)
	(Surname year, page number/s)
Footnote/Endnote	4. Matthew Wilhelm Kapell and John Shelton Lawrence, eds. <u>Finding the Force of the Star Wars Franchise: Fans, Merchandise and Critics</u>, (New York: Peter Lang, 2006), 133
	4. Editor 1 Name in full and Editor 2 Name in full, eds. *Title of book in italics* or <u>underlined</u>, (Place: Publisher, year), page number/s
Bibliography	Kapell, Matthew Wilhelm and John Shelton Lawrence, eds. <u>Finding the Force of the Star Wars Franchise: Fans, Merchandise and Critics</u>. New York: Peter Lang, 2006.
	Ed 1 Surname, Ed 1 First name/s and Ed 2 First name/s Ed 2 Surname, eds. *Title in italics* or <u>underlined</u>. Place: Publisher, year.

Note: in the above example the reference was taken from one of the editors (Lawrence). The following example informs you of how to cite a chapter that appears in an edited book.

Chapter in edited book

Type of reference	Harvard APA
In-text	(Porter, 2006, p.110)
	(Author of chapter's surname, year, page number/s)
How it should look in the bibliography	Porter, J.E. (2006). "I Am a Jedi": *Star Wars* Fandom, Religious Belief, and the 2001 Census. In M. W. Kapell & J. S. Lawrence (Eds.), *Finding the Force of the Star Wars Franchise: Fans, Merchandise and Critics* (pp. 95–112). New York: Peter Lang.
	Author of chapter, Initials (year). Title of chapter not in italics. In Initial of first editor, followed by surname, & Initial of second editor followed by surname (Eds.), *Title in italics* (pp. start and end pages of chapter). Place: Publisher.

Type of reference	MLA
In-text	(Porter 110)
	(Author of chapter surname page number/s)
Bibliography	Porter, Jennifer E. "'I Am a Jedi': *Star Wars* Fandom, Religious Belief, and the 2001 Census." <u>Finding the Force of the Star Wars Franchise: Fans, Merchandise and Critics</u>. Eds. Matthew Wilhelm Kapell and John Shelton Lawrence. New York: Peter Lang, 2006. 95–112.

Author's surname, followed by first name. "Title of chapter." *Title of book in italics* or underlined. Eds. Name of first editor followed by surname and name of second editor followed by surname. Place: Publisher, year. Page numbers of chapter.

Type of reference	**Chicago**
In-text	(Porter 2006, 110)
	(Author of chapter's surname, page number/s)
Footnote/ Endnote	6. Jennifer E. Porter, "'I Am a Jedi': *Star Wars* Fandom, Religious Belief, and the 2001 Census." In <u>Finding the Force of the Star Wars Franchise: Fans, Merchandise and Critics,</u> ed. Matthew Wilhelm Kapell and John Shelton Lawrence (New York: Peter Lang, 2006), 110.
	6. Author of chapter first name followed by surname, "Title of chapter." In *Title of book in italics* or <u>underlined</u> ed. Full names of first editor and second editor (Place: Publisher, year), page number/s.
Bibliography	Porter, Jennifer E. "'I Am a Jedi': *Star Wars* Fandom, Religious Belief, and the 2001 Census." In <u>Finding the Force of the Star Wars Franchise: Fans, Merchandise and Critics</u>, ed. Matthew Wilhelm Kapell and John Shelton Lawrence, 95–112. New York: Peter Lang, 2006.
	Author of chapter surname, first names. "Title of chapter." In *Title of book in italics* or <u>underlined</u>, ed. Full names of first editor and second editor, page numbers of entire chapter. Place: Publisher, year.

123

Journal articles

Type of reference Harvard APA

In-text

(Hark, 1976, p.4)

(Surname, year, page.number/s)

How it should look in the bibliography

Hark, I. R. (1976). The Visual Politics of *The Adventures of Robin Hood. The Journal of Popular Film* 5(1), 3–17.

Surname, Initials. (year). Title not in italics. *Title of journal in italics*, volume (issue number), start and end page numbers of article.

Type of reference MLA

In-text

(Hark 4)

(Surname page number/s)

Bibliography

Hark, Ina Rae. "The Visual Politics of *The Adventures of Robin Hood*." The Journal of Popular Film 5.1 (1976): 3–17.

Surname, first names. "Title of article." *Title of journal in italics* or underlined, volume. issue number (year): start and end page numbers of article.

Type of reference Chicago

In-text

(Hark 1976, 4)

(Surname year, page number/s)

Type of reference	Chicago
Footnote/Endnote	2. Ina Rae Hark, "The Visual Politics of *The Adventures of Robin Hood.*" <u>The Journal of Popular Film</u> 5, no.1 (1976): 3–17
	2. Author's full name, "Title of article." *Title of journal in italics* or <u>underlined</u> volume, no.issue (year): start and end page numbers of article
Bibliography	Hark, Ina Rae. "The Visual Politics of The Adventures of Robin Hood." <u>The Journal of Popular Film</u> 5, no.1 (1976): 3–17
	Surname, first name/s. "Title of article." *Title of journal in italics* or <u>underlined</u> volume, no. issue (year): start and end page numbers of article

Web pages

Type of reference	Harvard APA
In-text	(Pilgrim, para 8)
	(Surname, paragraph number)
How it should look in the bibliography	Pilgrim, D. (2000). *The Tragic Mulatto Myth*. Retrieved April 25, 2008 from http://jimcrow.museum/
	Surname, Initials. (year). *Title in italics*. Retrieved Month date, year from internet address

Type of reference	MLA
In-text	(Pilgrim)
	(Surname)
	If there is no author ("The Tragic Mulatto Myth")
	("Name of web page")
Bibliography	Pilgrim, D. "The Tragic Mulatto Myth" 2000. http://jimcrow.museum/ (25 April 2008)
	Surname, Initials. "Title" date of publication. (If available) web address (date of access)

Type of reference	Chicago
In-text	(Pilgrim)
	(Surname)
Footnote/Endnote	5. David Pilgrim, "The Tragic Mulatto Myth." (2000), http://jimcrow. museum/ (Accessed April 25th, 2008)
	5. Full name, "Title of web page." (year), web address (Accessed Month day, year)
Bibliography	Pilgrim, David. "The Tragic Mulatto Myth." (2000), http://jimcrow. museum/ (Accessed April 25th, 2008)
	Surname, First name/s. "Title of web page." (year), web address (Accessed Month day, year)

Note: online web pages and journal articles often do not have page numbers. When citing a reference from an online source you need to identify what paragraph your quote or paraphrase comes from.

Films

Type of reference	Harvard APA
In-text	(Lucas, 1977)
	(Surname, Year)
How it should look in the bibliography	Lucas, G. (Director). (1977). *Star Wars* [Motion Picture]. United States: Twentieth Century-Fox.
	Surname, Initial (Director). (year). *Title in italics* [Motion Picture]. Country of origin: Studio.

Type of reference	MLA
In-text	(<u>Star Wars</u>)
	(*Title of film in italics* or <u>underlined</u>)
Bibliography	<u>Star Wars.</u> Dir. George Lucas. Perf. Harrison Ford, Mark Hamill and Carrie Fisher. Twentieth Century-Fox, 1977
	Title in italics or <u>underlined</u>. Dir. Director. Perf. List key performers. Studio, Date

Type of reference	Chicago
In-text	Lucas, <u>Star Wars</u>
	Surname, *Title in Italics* or <u>Underlined</u>

Type of reference	Chicago
Footnote/Endnote	22. George Lucas, Director, <u>Star Wars</u>, 1977.
	22. Full name, Director, *Title in Italics* or <u>Underlined</u>, year.
Bibliography	<u>Star Wars</u>. Directed by George Lucas. 1977. United States: Twentieth Century-Fox.
	Title in Italics or <u>Underlined</u>. Directed by full name. Year. Country of origin: Studio.

Note: if you are struggling to find production details for films then you can always check imdb.com, although this is not regarded as an academic site, so best not to reference it.

The above examples should be used as a basic guideline. There is a great deal of contradictory information regarding correct referencing and in-text citations that is available on-line. Different universities have different rules regarding full stops and commas or capitalization. You may find that the illustrations above do not comply with the rules and regulations imposed by your university. Therefore, it is very important that you familiarise yourself with the style and format that will be used in your assessments as you do not want to lose marks for referencing.

SEMINAR ACTIVITY

The following extract is taken from an online article by Flanagan (2007); the extract that follows it is from a fictional student essay. In this activity identify instances of plagiarism and poor scholarship in the student essay, in its use of Flanagan's original piece.

Flanagan Article

The massive influence that the Western has exerted on world film culture has led to the form being spoken of in terms of "genre imperialism" (Maltby 123). Initial innovations in Western form went hand in hand with the development of the cinema as a narrative medium, as is evinced in *The Great Train Robbery*. Edwin S. Porter's 1903 film, with its depiction of temporally parallel story lines, "defined the limits of a certain kind of narrative construction" that would become Hollywood's fundamental storytelling mode (Musser 256). Later, the iconographic apparatus of the Western would ensure its status as the perfect conduit for the demonstration of technological advances such as widescreen, with the genre exemplifying, for André Bazin, "the American film par excellence" (140). However, all empires, even those of genre, are built on a kind of oppression; when do innovations become limitations? The marginalization of the racial and sexual other in the classical Western, when viewed from a perspective of 2007, rightly problematizes our political reading of the genre. The rigid ideological character of the genre is linked, in some way, to the attitude displayed by the films to history: the makers of history – the white males – are glorified; those who live under its terms – everybody else – are all but removed from the picture. Representational strategies, of course, play a huge part in the promulgation of this myth, and within the Western aesthetic a decisive role is played by time/space formulations that can be productively analysed using Mikhail Bakhtin's concept of "chronotope".

Student Essay

It is the contention of this essay that the massive influence that the Western has exerted on world film culture has led to the form being spoken of in terms of genre imperialism. The first Western being *The Great Train Robbery*. Many years later, the

129

iconography of the Western would ensure its status as the perfect model for the demonstration of technological advances such as widescreen. However, as M. Flanagan says "The marginalization of the racial and sexual other in the classical Western, when viewed from a perspective of 2007, rightly problematizes our political reading of the genre." His work seeks to realign notions of bakhtin's concept of chronotope to reappraise the Western in the contexts of contemporary cinema.

FINAL ADVICE

- Collect your references, keep a record in a separate bibliography.
- Always check your referencing style guide for help with citing your work.
- Become familiar with your field of study – read more than your set texts, read the journals that are published regularly.
- Make research a part of your day (perhaps start a reading group)?
- Look towards your dissertation from the first year.
- Develop a capacity for independent learning.
- Organise your time.
- Invest in your degree (buy books).
- Remember, the internet does not hold the answer.

WORKS CITED (ACCORDING TO THE HARVARD APA REFERENCING SYSTEM)

American Psychological Association. (2005). *Concise Rules of APA Style*. Washington: American Psychological Association.

Bock, H. (1988). Academic Literacy: Starting Point or Goal? In G. Taylor, B. Ballard, V. Beasley, H. Bock, J. Clanchy, &

P. Nightingale (Eds.). *Literacy by Degrees* (pp. 24–41). Milton Keynes: Open University Press.

The Chicago Manual of Style (15th ed.). (2003). Chicago: The University of Chicago Press.

D'Andrea, V., & Gosling, D. (2005). *Improving Teaching and Learning in Higher Education: A Whole Institution Approach*. Maidenhead: Open University Press.

Flanagan, M. (2007). Re-Making Time: Chronotopes of the West in *Lone Star* (1996) and *The Searchers* (1956). *Reconstruction: Studies in Contemporary Culture* 7(3). Retrieved December 12, 2007, from http://reconstruction.eserver.org/073/flanagan.shtml

Gibaldi, J. (2003). *MLA Handbook for Writers of Research Papers* (6th ed.). New York: The Modern Language Association of America.

Hendricks, M., & Quinn, L. (2000). Teaching Referencing as an Introduction to Epistemological Empowerment. *Teaching in Higher Education* 5(4), 447–57.

Jenkins, H. (1992). *Textual Poachers: Television Fans and Participatory Culture*. New York: Routledge.

Mann, S. J. (2000). The Student's Experience of Reading. *Higher Education* 39(3), 297–317.

Martin, P. W. (2003). Key Aspects of Teaching and Learning in Arts, Humanities and Social Sciences. In H. Fry, S. Ketteridge, & S. Marshall (Eds.). *A Handbook for Teaching & Learning in Higher Education: Enhancing Academic Practice* (pp. 301–23). London: Routledge Farmer.

Sandvoss, C. (2005). *Fans: The Mirror of Consumption*. Cambridge: Polity Press.

Uemlianin, I. A. (2000). Engaging Text: Assessing Paraphrase and Understanding. *Studies in Higher Education* 25(3), 347–58.

Chapter 14

Writing on film

Laurie Ede

INTRODUCTION

Film students are often stereotyped as people who spend all of their time going to the pictures and watching DVDs. Clearly, the film scholar should regard films as their most important resource. The movie is to the film academic what the novel is to the student of literature and, considered in isolation, it can offer clues on a range of subjects, including:

- The contemporary cultural and social scene (i.e. the state of a culture or society at the time of the film's manufacture).
- Notions of gender, class and race.
- The artistic preoccupations of the filmmaker(s).
- Aesthetic developments in film-making.

But complete Film Studies cannot be a matter of pure textual analysis. Films do not appear out of thin air. Some writers see them as the embodiment of desire; on the part of their makers (as in *auteur* analyses of films) or of particular constituencies of viewers (as in recent fan-based approaches to movies). Other thinkers on film insist that movies should be thought of primarily as commodities, the products of cultural entrepreneurs who seek to control and shape desire in order to maximise sales (genre analysts will often take this line). Such debates cannot be reconciled purely by watching films. Take, for instance, the first point in the list above,

133

concerning a film's apparent reflection of contemporary social and cultural circumstances. Clearly, we cannot adjudge a film's representation of wider trends unless we know something about its specific social and historical context. For example, it is often said that Action Films of the 1980s (the *Die Hards*, *Rambos* and so on) reflected the contemporary political scene in America. This may be true, but in order to know for sure we would have to consider the socio-political context of the time, as defined by the Reagan presidency. We would also have to think about all of the points of mediation and slippage which rest between contemporary society and culture and the making of any film. Movies are never a pure reflection of their times; rather they *refract* society, as they attempt to meet public expectation and thus find a market.

So we can see that Film Studies is not just a matter of looking at films; the diligent film scholar will take account of both *text* (the film itself) and *context*. In practice, the contextual evidences are often written and they may include:

- Newspaper articles
- Academic journal articles
- Academic books
- Film reviews
- Popular books on films
- Biographies and autobiographies
- Scripts

There is a real art to deriving the full value from printed texts and it often takes years to acquire. Materials about films, no less than the films themselves, are written in particular ways for particular readerships. For example, a film script is written for the people involved in the production of the film. By this token, it can provide us with valuable evidence of the original intentions of the writer and/or director (and perhaps provide an illuminating contrast with the finished film). Other kinds of printed texts require astute handling on the part of the film scholar. Particular problems accrue to the reading of critical accounts of films. Broadly, we can divide film criticism into two camps: *popular* and *academic*. The former pieces of writing are often used as *primary* sources; i.e. original, contemporary materials which are marshalled by the film scholar. In contrast, academic articles are usually considered to be *secondary* sources, where the raw evidences have already been reconstituted by a film thinker. But all of this begs one central question:

> How can we tell the difference between popular and academic writing on films?

This is the nub of this chapter. As we will see, this question has important implications for the evaluation of written film evidences.

SPOT THE DIFFERENCE

Academics are oddly mute on issues to do with film criticism – you'll search in vain in basic film text books for any critical remarks concerning the critics themselves (save for the odd caveat on writers who became film directors, such as the progenitors of the French and British New Waves). This absence is problematic, because it tends to render critics and their works as transparent or, worse, invisible. The silence over the functioning of the critic is also regrettable because it obscures the wide variety of approaches to film critique.

The astute film academic will want to avail him/herself of the full range of written evidences – all sorts of things can tell us something about films and their audiences. But to do this effectively, we need first to be able to distinguish between different kinds of written texts. As a starting point, this necessitates some appreciation of markets and audiences. We can begin to grasp this point if we consider the respective readerships of popular and academic film critique.

135

Popular film critics make their living in whole or in part from reviewing films (or at least that's the idea). Their reviews and associated articles may be found in the following places:

- Newspapers (broadsheet, tabloid and popular 'Red Top' tabloids such as *The Sun* and the *Daily Mirror*)
- Popular magazines (e.g. *Total Film*, *Empire*)
- TV and radio review programmes
- Film publicity materials (e.g. press handouts)

Academic critics typically earn their primary living from working in universities and other places of learning. Their work is published in the following places:

- Academic journals (such as *Screen*, *Wide Angle*, *Journal of British Cinema and Television*)
- Books and collections, published by specialist academic publishers
- Academic websites (e.g. *Screening the Past*, *Scope*)

Of course, this is a crude schema. For one thing, the lines are sometimes blurred between academic and popular film magazines; for example, the British Film Institute's journal *Sight & Sound* attempts to appeal to both popular and academic audiences (the articles and reviews are written by both scholars and journalists).

Erstwhile demarcations between popular and academic film critique are also being obscured on the world wide web by sites such as Harry Knowles's *Ain't it Cool?* and the Amazon-owned *Internet Movie Database.*

In the end, the film critic is often best identified by his/her works. We understand that we are in the presence of a piece of popular or academic work by clues in the text itself, such as the themes which are explored, the sentence structures and the register of the language.

. . . That last point is very important.

136

SOME THOUGHTS ON REGISTER

The notion of 'registers' of language comes from the world of linguistics. Linguists argue that language is culturally and socially specific. More than this, they suggest that people use certain modes of language in specific kinds of social situations. To cite an obvious example, here's an extract from a solicitor's letter:

> '2.2. Where the grant or exercise of any rights or reservations herein referred to would otherwise contravene the rule against perpetuities the same shall be limited to those granted or becoming exercisable within the period of Eighty years from the date of the Lease (the "perpetuity period").'

The meaning of this is unclear to anyone unfamiliar with legal jargon; what it says: *I'm a solicitor and you're not*. This is apparent not just from the professional language employed ('reservations', 'herein', 'perpetuities') but from the tone and rhythm of the paragraph. The clause has a breathless quality which defies ordinary rules of grammar and syntax; look closely and you'll find not a single comma. In this way, it seems to hark back to an old, implicitly august, style of written English which is quite distinct from everyday styles of speech. Of course, this is the idea; in some sense, legal speak (legalese) appears to have an authority which is bestowed upon it by history; we can only feel in awe of it.

Numerous philosophers throughout the years – from Michel Foucault to Michael Halliday to Pierre Bourdieu – have written of the relationships between language and power. Professionals in particular are deemed to use words to establish their difference from others and thus reinstate their right to social and economic privilege. Solicitors are not the only culprits. All kinds of people use words as weapons or, to use the term favoured by social scientists, derive power and prestige from their selective *discourse*. Take, for example, this oft-invoked phrase from Bourdieu:

'Taste classifies and it classifies the classifier'

Bourdieu wants to show here how people deploy nebulous standards of taste as the means of underscoring their own social power. Thus, for example, the wine expert may use the jargon of his trade ('vanilla topnotes', 'blackberry undertones') as the means of simultaneously figuring his own taste – classifying himself – and establishing his difference from the rest of us.

These thoughts on register and discourse are highly pertinent to the study of film. No less than the wine expert or the solicitor, film critics use language as the means of defining themselves. This has important implications for the evaluation of printed texts of all kinds. In order to know the value of a piece of printed evidence, we have to understand its own context of production (i.e. the purpose of the piece in question, the market that it addresses) and we also need to attend to the register(s) of language employed.

The extracts below explore the same film, the science-fiction epic *Artificial Intelligence: A.I.* (2001), but they vary widely in tone, structure and purpose. *A.I.* is an interesting film to study from the perspective of critical discourse. It was produced and directed by Steven Spielberg, the man who, more than any other, has come to be associated with the big-budget blockbuster (his *Jaws* initiated this marketing technique). But *A.I.* had serious intentions. To begin with, the script was derived from a story by the esteemed sci-fi writer Brian Aldiss. Moreover, the project was suggested to Spielberg by the famous auteur-director Stanley Kubrick. The air of gravitas which surrounded *A.I.* affected much of the press that surrounded it. A number of academics found it gave 'food for thought' for their theses as based, variously, on cybernetics, postmodernism and (as below) Freudian psychoanalysis. Popular and 'quality' newspaper critics also felt the need to engage with the film's high aims. Nonetheless, we can still perceive differences in the approaches taken to the film and the language deployed in every instance.

138

To begin with, read through the three short extracts and then work through the seminar questions as provided.

EXTRACT ONE

A. I. persistently invokes a number of psychic discourses and responses, showing David's 'mother' at one point on the toilet reading *Freud on Women*. The scene itself is reminiscent of Freud's famous admission of a childhood memory (recounted in *Freud on Women*) of his searching for his mother in a wardrobe and crying until he found her. In Spielberg's scene, David opens the bathroom door on his mother and, smiling, says 'I found you'. In line with the way in which Freudian discourses are deployed to allude to *A. I.*'s cultural and aesthetic engagements, Spielberg's previous flirtations with Oedipal complexes (*The Sugarland Express* [1974], E. T. [1982], *Empire of the Sun* [1987] and *Hook* [1991]) are noticeably developed in this film into full-blown speculations on the construction of the subconscious and portraits of maternity as a point of origin in an age where the 'original' is purportedly nowhere to be found. As I will demonstrate, the tension between the 'original' and its derivative, or the sequel, informs the film's portrait of virtual subjectivity. Perhaps more pointed, however, is the film's construction of reflective surfaces and the circle as symbols of David's psychological development. I go on to discuss the film's representations of the subconscious and subjectivity in terms of the Freudian and Lacanian theories it appears to invoke.

Jess-Cook, C. (2006). Virtualizing the Real: sequelization and secondary memory in Steven Spielberg's *Artificial Intelligence: A. I.*. *Screen*. 47(3), 347.

EXTRACT TWO

In theory, Kubrick should play the salty Lennon to Spielberg's sucrose McCartney. Or, to put it another way: Stanley provides the hi-tech high concept and Steven gives it the big, beating heart. But it turns out like George Bernard Shaw's joke to the beautiful young woman who wanted to breed with him: what if the baby gets my body and your brains? AI winds up with Kubrick's empathy and Spielberg's intellectual muscle. It's a lethal combination.

For a start, it's an almost laughably creaky museum piece. If Kubrick had made this 30 years ago as the story of a 'star child' whose spiritual trajectory spans thousands of years, it might have been stunning. Instead he made 2001: A Space Odyssey. If Spielberg had made it 20 years ago, about an adorable, unearthly creature estranged from human love, that too might have been stunning. Instead he made E T.

Poor AI is orphaned by the times. In any case, the whole idea of the robot as the avatar of future existence is about as cutting-edge as the Post Office Tower. As an issue it has been rendered obsolete by biotech, cloning, the human genome. As for the furniture, the set dressings, the fixtures and fittings: uh, futuristic? Creamy white decor, laundry bag-trolleys, groovy circular staircases: very Stanley Kubrick, very Sanderson.

Bradshaw, P. (2001, September 21). A.I. Artificial Intelligence. *Guardian,* p. 27.

EXTRACT THREE

AI is really three films rolled into one: Awfully Irritating, Amazingly Ingenious and Absolutely Inspired. And if that's not enough, you get 'em all in the last 20 minutes!

The result is an emotional rollercoaster leaving you Absolutely Infuriated, Utterly Enthralled and Absolutely Knackered.

This is without doubt the strangest, most important movie Steven Spielberg has made – and some scenes are his finest work.

Stanley Kubrick was to have been exec producer for this film, so it has the cold focus of his best work allied with the rich fairytale feel of Spielberg masterpieces.

The Vegas-On-Acid look of the Rouge City fleshpot, where robot hookers of both sexes ply their trades, is simply astounding.

And drowned New York, with its weird undersea fairground, is Awe Inspiring too.

Emotion

The Oscar-deserving performances from Jude Law and Sixth Sense star Haley Joel Osment are the best Spielberg has ever teased from his actors.

The raw emotion packed into this film is unbearable at times. Somehow you actually feel the uncontrollable longing of a child torn from his mother. Yes, it's that strong.

Mind you, some of it stinks. Entire scenes are even worse than the vomit-inducing torments Spielberg served up in Hook.

Lowlights include the robot-smashing WWF-style shenanigans at the Flesh Fair, when obsolete androids are blasted out of cannons or drenched with acid. Just like Kubrick's 2001, you need to let this one wash over your mind – leaving you highly amused, slightly abused and totally confused. See it. Argue about it. Fail to understand it.

Ross, P. (2001, September 18). Awe Inspiring but Spielberg epic is Awfully Irritating Too. *News of the World*, p. 18.

SEMINAR EXERCISE

Working with a partner, take 30 minutes to work through the article in greater depth, considering the following questions.

1   (Extract One) Which words characterise this extract as an academic piece?

2   (Extract One) How do the themes of this piece differ from the other two extracts?

3   (Extract Two) How would you describe the tone of this article (ironic? serious? reverential?). How does this differ from the other extracts?

4   (Extract Two) Why does the writer include cultural references outside the film?

5   (Extract Three) How would you describe the rhythm of the writing? Why does Paul Ross write in this way?

6   (Extract Three) Can you find any clichés here? How are they used?

At the end of the half hour, your seminar leader will invite each group to respond to one of the questions. You should be prepared to talk for 2–3 minutes on any of the themes and be ready also to contribute to the wider group discussion.

WHAT'S THE POINT OF ALL OF THIS?

To begin with, we might recall the thoughts of that noted philosopher, the soul singer Marvin Gaye: 'People say believe half of what you see, Son, and none of what you hear'.[1] The purpose of discourse

1   M. Gaye, 'I Heard It Through the Grapevine' (1968, N.Whitfield/ B.Strong, Stone Agate Music).

analysis is to demonstrate that the truth is relative; relative to what people feel compelled to say and relative also to what people are able or prepared to understand. Put simply, one should never accept something merely because it's placed on a printed page. At the same time, the film student should be aware of the relative value of different kinds of printed evidence.

The foregoing seminar exercise was intended to take you from a state of gut-feeling to a position of detailed knowledge. In *deconstructing* the three extracts you have hopefully learned something about the ways in which writers use language to position the reader and to get things across to an anticipated audience.

What can you do with such evidence? This really depends upon the problem that lies before you. Throughout your degree studies you will produce various forms of written assignments, including essays and a final year dissertation. The full versions of the seminar extracts could prove to be helpful in a number of contexts. For example:

Extract One

This article could yield fruit if you were producing a dissertation on issues of subjectivity in science fiction. It also has some important points to make about the continuing relevance, as the writer sees it, of post-structuralist theory (of which Lacanian psychoanalysis forms a part). Implicitly, Carolyn Jess-Cook's analysis also suggests that blockbusters can be thoughtful.

Extract Two

This contains some good background information concerning the making of *A.I.* It also says something about the relative status of Kubrick and Spielberg (in the not un-typical view of a middle-brow critic). Most obviously, the piece could provide an interesting quote or two for a project on *A.I* or the Spielberg oeuvre.

Extract Three

Paul Ross's comments provide good evidence of the popular reception afforded to Spielberg's attempted grand opus. They would sit well in a project or essay on the theme of modern film science fiction. Stylistically, this piece also typifies the pithy style of recent red-top film critique. A film and journalism student could make effective use of such pieces for a project on popular film discourse.

The above thoughts are not meant to be definitive. As time goes on, you will develop an expanded sense of the uses that can be made of the full range of printed evidences. In all likelihood, you will also acquire a more sophisticated grasp of the subtleties of discourse analysis.

A FINAL THOUGHT

This article has carried an implicit message to do with the universality of discourse; I have wanted to show that every kind of writing on films is determined to some degree by a self-conscious awareness of the intended readership. Nothing is discourse-free . . . and that includes this chapter.

Perhaps you have been aware of my own authorial voice as you have read this article? If so, you should take your rightful place at the top of the class. Sincerely, I have tried to write this in an open and friendly way, but I may have fallen into old academic habits. There is some jargon here ('auteur', 'discourse', 'register'); at times, I make use of well-known theorists (Bourdieu, Foucault) in a manner which you may think is designed to endorse my own professional status; my references to the supposed discipline of 'discourse analysis' could also be interpreted as lending uncritical support to a contested branch of social science method. It's up to you what you think. The key point about Film Studies – and any other Humanities discipline – is that you should uncover evidences to support your own ideas. Printed materials of all kinds form an important part of the academic mix.

Chapter 15

Making the most of feedback

Laurel Forster

PREPARATION

1   Bring along to the session two or three marked essays, with the assessment sheets.
2   Note down three effective feedback comments you have received in the past, and three comments which you did not find helpful. Think about how these comments make you feel.

INTRODUCTION

The feedback you receive on your work is key to the progression in your studies and hence your success at university. It has been argued that 'Feedback on performance is [. . .] the cornerstone of all learning' (Orrell, 2006, p. 441). Assignment feedback is the main form of academic support from tutors, and vital to the learning process, so it is really important to read and understand the comments about your work. All feedback should be viewed as a means to improving the quality of your studies at university, in terms of both your critical thinking and your written output. If a tutor has made a comment and drawn something to your attention, it is with the intention of helping you perhaps specifically in your next assignment or more generally in your overall degree work. It is therefore important to take careful notice of the remarks made. If you don't understand the comments then make arrangements to see your tutor to discuss them.

WHAT IS FEEDBACK?

There are three main types of feedback you will receive from your tutors:

1   Immediate oral responses to views in seminars.
2   Individual one-on-one advice in tutorials.
3   Formal written feedback on essay and/or assignment.

Feedback is everything you receive from your tutors regarding your work. It may include a mark for the assignment, written comments on an assessment sheet and possibly a tutorial conversation. In addition, you may receive some peer evaluation and even have access to a second marker's comments. It could also take the form of a tutor response in a group seminar session. It may be formal in tone using the language of the unit learning objectives, or informal as in a friendly tutorial.

Feedback is instruction in how to improve your studies and work, and is one of the most important aspects of your degree. It is individually tailored and specific to your work and, most importantly, feedback is a process in which you must participate if you want to benefit from the advice of your tutors, and make advances in your work.

UNDERSTANDING THE FEEDBACK PROCESS

It is important to understand how feedback works, and to shed any negative views. It is quite simple really: no-one comes to university expecting to know everything already, and guidance regarding your strengths and weaknesses from your tutors is one way to learn and improve. Another, of course, is your own significant efforts in your reading and studies. It is vital to see any form of criticism not as judgement but as one of the constructive processes at work in the progression towards the final outcome of your degree.

Why then do a number of students find it difficult to deal with feedback? For some it is the seeming shift in relationship with their tutor. The person who was 'assisting' you in seminars and lectures is now the person 'passing judgement' on you when marking your assignments (Higgins *et al.*, 2001, p. 273). Such shifts between equality and authority may seem strange, but become easier to understand when you see university as a place where we are *all* still learning. Most lecturers regard themselves as continuing to develop their expertise in a number of academic fields, i.e. they are still studying. However, through their extended studies and publications they are now in a position to help you develop your academic interests and skills. The key to understanding this dual role, which may be very different to some school systems, is to see your tutor both as a facilitator, someone who encourages you to develop your own academic interests and abilities, as well as someone who imparts knowledge through lectures, seminars and assessment. Remember that it is a significant part of your tutor's job to criticise and evaluate your work in order to help you improve.

Another lesser-known aspect of the process is to get 'feed forward' before you get 'feedback'. The idea of feeding forward into a piece of work is where a tutor and student discuss and clarify an assignment before it is finished or perhaps even started (Higgins, 2001, p. 274.). This is part of the process where you can be quite proactive. For instance, you can ask questions about the assignment to make sure you have completely understood all that is required and exactly how it will be assessed. What do the learning outcomes specify; what kind of approach is your tutor expecting? Similarly, you can feed forward into your essays through your seminars. You

149

can test understanding of your reading by bringing points up when making your seminar contributions. Seeing the response to your comments in this safe testing ground will help you determine whether you are reading the appropriate material and understanding it in the right way.

YOUR CONTRIBUTION TO THE PROCESS

Receiving feedback can be an emotional experience: not only do you have to deal with someone else's comments on your work, but you have to cope with your own expectations of yourself too. A really good way of overcoming these emotional hurdles is to see yourself as a significant part of the feedback process.

Try to be systematic in dealing with feedback.

- Read each comment carefully and look again at your work, especially those areas referred to directly.
- Some comments will be summative, i.e. it will reflect on a specific piece of submitted work, and some will be formative, i.e. looking forward to or helping you 'form', and improve, your next piece of work. Both types of feedback are useful for your future work.
- If you seem to have misunderstood something go back to the text book or watch the film again.
- Make sure you understand your tutor's comments in the context of your own writing. This is a most powerful learning process, so set aside time when you are able to concentrate. A quick glance at the tutor's comments as you rush to your next lecture is not enough.
- Think carefully about how you might have improved these aspects of your work and how you might avoid those pitfalls later.
- Work on those aspects which need improvement: perhaps rewrite a paragraph or two, do some more reading and take

further notes in the areas where weaknesses have been pointed out.

- If your problems lie with study skills such as essay structure or referencing, then seek help through the university's learning support unit. Often there will be specific university leaflets on these aspects of degree-level work.
- If you really cannot understand where you have gone wrong, go and ask you tutor. But do not go empty-handed; take along your marked essay and some notes from your reading to discuss.
- Take careful note of all the positive comments. These are your strengths and will be significant in your success at university. Know what these are and build on them.

The most important person in the feedback process is you. Unless you carefully read and understand your feedback, and reflect upon it at length, you are not participating properly in the process. No matter how much you would rather just forget about a bad mark, you must read the comments and relate them to your assignment. Whether you are pleased with your mark or not, it is best to leave your essay for a few days after seeing the mark and deal properly with the feedback later, when the emotion has disappeared from the situation.

Read through all the comments carefully and allow yourself to learn. If you feel awkward about doing this, just pretend you are reading feedback for a friend who has similar inhibitions. When you see how valuable an exercise it is, you will wonder why you haven't done this before. However you achieve it, you must be objective. Consider using a table such as the one on page 152.

By identifying areas where tutors consistently comment, you will start to see where your weaknesses and strengths lie. This is very useful information as you can then seek specific assistance to help you improve in areas of assignment work where it is most needed.

Essay title	Content and scope	Expression of ideas	Quality of research	Essay structure	Spelling, punctuation, grammar	Referencing

SEMINAR EXERCISE 1

Taking the three essays and mark sheets you have brought to the session, complete the table above.

- Note down any specific or detailed comments by tutors.
- Note remarks that reflect strengths and weaknesses.
- Write down any patterns that emerge from the positive and negative feedback you have received.
- Consider how you might improve these aspects of your work.

Make a date in your diary this week to follow up the specific areas you need to improve; e.g. visit the library to take out a book on punctuation, or visit learning support to follow through on essay structure.

If you are unclear as to how to address some of the issues identified in this process then seek advice and help from the tutor or your university's academic support unit.

BE YOUR OWN BEST CRITIC

By the time you progress through your degree in years two and especially in year three, you should be able to provide a critique of your own writing and that of other people. It is best to perform the two tasks of writer and critic on different days as they require different approaches.

If you can anticipate potential problems with your work and deal with them before handing in the assignment, then your work and hopefully your grades will improve. In tutorials students often say, 'I always lose marks for . . . ', which of course means that they could have anticipated the criticism and improved their work beforehand. Always hand in the very best work you can, don't wait for feedback from the tutor to tell you something you already know. As your work moves on, so will your tutor's commentary.

The above exercise is designed to give you an insight into the ways in which degree-level work is assessed. It will give you an idea of what tutors look for in an undergraduate essay. It aims to help you understand that the giving and receiving of feedback is a process designed to assist you in improving your work. It is important to understand that feedback is about a flow of information, the variable student response, and the huge responsibility of the tutor to give appropriate and helpful feedback will help you to understand feedback for what it is: a significant learning process.

THE LAST WORD

Remember, feedback is for your benefit, no-one else's. The feedback you receive from your tutor is not the end of the process. The end is when you have reflected, re-read and reconsidered your work in the light of that feedback. Only when you have absorbed the feedback comments and evaluated what has been said about your progress, can that particular feedback cycle come to an end. You control this, not the tutor. Stay in control and make the most of your feedback.

Chapter 16

Exam preparation

Emma Dyson and Paul Spicer

INTRODUCTION

Exams for many students are the most stressful form of assessment. The exam hall environment, the time factor and the degree of preparation needed all make it a challenging proposition. However, exams serve several purposes: they encourage clarity of thinking, test your ability to develop an argument and provide an opportunity to demonstrate your knowledge on a subject. Fortune may favour the brave, but exams favour the well-prepared. This chapter aims to help you in your preparation.

A/AS-LEVEL TO DEGREE LEVEL: DO EXAMS CHANGE?

In terms of setting, expected behaviour and allocated time periods, there is not much difference between exams sat at school or college. You will be assessed on topics you have covered on your course. However, there are key differences in how the questions are prepared, and how you are expected to respond to them. A/AS-Level exams are created and assessed by national and regional exam boards, whereas university exams are created and assessed by university lecturers. Therefore it is usual practice for your unit/module co-ordinator to write the exam questions, and be responsible for the marking. Your answers should show a greater depth of individual research, a willingness to engage with specific theoretical debates and an analytical perspective. The expectations at university are that your answers are less descriptive than was previously acceptable, and that you demonstrate more in-depth understanding, rather than simply reproducing information.

TYPES OF EXAM

Exams as a form of assessment have changed over time. Traditionally, a degree was assessed in the final year of study by exams, sometimes known as 'finals'. Nowadays most universities favour ongoing assessment rather than a single pressurised examination period. This is why research projects, essays and other forms of assessment now exist alongside exams. There are, of course, different types of exams and what is expected of you will change depending on the particular method of assessment. Here are a few examples.

The Unseen Exam

This is possibly the most challenging form of exam. You may be fearful of not understanding what the question is asking of you, and you may also be worried that the exam will feature topics that you have not revised.

The Seen or Open Exam

In this case questions are given in advance. This provides you with plenty of time to revise topics that interest you, but also means your answers should be detailed and show evidence of your research.

The Open Book Exam

This format allows you to bring key texts into the examination hall. This type of exam is traditionally associated with other disciplines, such as English Literature; however, this type of exam may be relevant for modules such as Film Theory.

It is always a good idea to check with your lecturer beforehand to see whether notes can be taken into the exam. Some institutions allow a page of handwritten notes that must be handed in at the end along with your answers.

RULES, REGULATIONS AND ENTITLEMENTS

Once you know you have to sit an exam, find out what is expected of you; read your university's exam regulations. Check all your course materials. Every university has a list of expected behaviour and entitlements for exams that you should be aware of. These should be accessible via your university website as well as in hard copies.

- **Can I take in my bag?** You need to check the regulations and can always ask the invigilator. All mobiles should be switched off, and you may need to put your stationery in a clear plastic wallet or bag.
- **Do I need my student card?** Most universities insist you have your student or campus card or another form of recognised ID in order to sit an exam.
- **What do I do if I'm ill?** If you cannot make it to the exam you should contact the university straight away. Check your department's guidelines for reporting absence/illness. If you are unwell but still attend, advise the invigilator of your illness. After the exam investigate your institution's regulations regarding extenuating circumstances, and discuss these with your tutor. You may be required to provide medical evidence in support of your case.
- **What if I am taking medication?** If you are taking any prescribed medication that you feel may impair your responses, inform the invigilator and your tutor.
- **What do I do if I'm late for the exam?** Make sure you know what time you have to be in the exam hall, and ensure

that you arrive at least 15 minutes before it is due to start. If you are late because of circumstances beyond your control, inform someone as soon as you can. It's a good idea to find out who you can call, and have their name and number in case of emergencies. Most universities have regulations about how late you can be in entering an exam.

■ **What if I am coping with a disability or learning difficulties?** If you are registered with the university as having learning difficulties, or in need of extra support, you may be granted extra time, assistance, computer use, access to a dictionary, or be assessed in a separate room. These provisions need to be arranged in advance, so see what you are entitled to and contact the relevant staff.

REVISION METHODS AND PRACTICES

There are many ways of approaching revision, and you will find a formula that works best for you. Think about methods that you have used previously and consider which gave you the best results, and which did not really work for you.

Opposite you will find a chart which covers the key areas in planning your revision. We have chosen to present this information as a mindmap, which may also be a useful tool when revising for exams.

SEMINAR ACTIVITY

Write an exam question based on one of your university modules, and produce a plan that would help you revise.

Prediction

* Note down possible
  questions
* Take note when
  lecturers stress
  ideas as important
* Look at past papers
* Consider material
  covered in lectures
  and seminars

Organisation

* Do you have a
  complete set of
  notes?
* Can you access
  missing information?
* Make sure notes
  are organised and
  legible.
* Make detailed notes
  on key readings

REVISION

Revision style

* Rewrite notes –
  consider colour
  coding
* Use 'post-its' for
  key points
* Organise ideas with
  mind-maps
* Record notes into a
  Dictaphone
* Try group revision

Knowledge

* Familiarise yourself
  with film texts
* Check spellings
  (directors/characters)
* Know your
  production history
* Research social,
  economic and
  political context
* Be aware of formal,
  and thematic traits

TIME MANAGEMENT

Good time management is crucial to revision. It is always important to have a revision schedule and stick to it, whether this is an ongoing process throughout the semester or the period before the exam. Here are some tips:

■ At least a few weeks before the exam draw up a revision programme. Choose carefully the topics that you need to focus on and make sure that you allocate the appropriate amount of time to each area.

■ Make sure that you are familiar with the material and understand it.

■ Put time aside each week for revision. Two- or three-hour sessions may seem like a lot, but you will cover a substantial amount.

■ Work out the times when you are most productive for your revision, and make sure that you can work uninterrupted.

■ Make sure you take regular breaks and reward yourself when you've done your revision.

■ Don't leave revision to the last minute, as this will create additional stress and pressure.

STRESS AND EXAM NERVES

People can be affected by stress at different points in their lives, but exams tend to bring out a little stress in everyone. A lot of this can be countered by making sure you are comfortable with what you have to do and when you have to do it.

■ Make sure you know where the exam is being held. If you don't know where the building is find out well in advance.

■ Keep an eye on notice boards, email communications and information given in class regarding any possible changes relating to your exam.

- If stress is badly affecting you, consider alternative approaches to relaxation, such as herbal remedies, meditation, hypnotherapy, acupuncture or seek medical advice.
- Remember that your tutors are available to discuss any issues with.

THE NIGHT BEFORE THE EXAM

Preparation is key to doing well in exams. This checklist may help sort out a few last-minute preparations.

1 Make sure that your travel arrangements are in place and allow for delays.
2 It is a good idea to have a back-up plan in case you fail to wake up in time, e.g. set an additional alarm clock or arrange for a phone call from a friend or relative.
3 Prepare any items you may need for the exam the night before, such as texts or stationery.
4 Take time to wind down before bed, knowing you have done everything you can do. Try to get a good night's sleep.

THE DAY OF THE EXAM

You need to get to the exam *at least* 15 minutes before the exam is due to start so the invigilators have time to seat everyone and explain any regulations. While waiting outside, turn off your mobile phone and get everything that you need ready – you may not be allowed to take your bag with you. Have your student card or another form of identification ready. While waiting, don't be tempted to predict the questions as this could knock your confidence.

DURING THE EXAM

When you get to your desk, fill out any cover sheets you are asked to. Don't turn over any papers, or write anything else. Remember that if you there is anything that you need to ask all you have to do is raise your hand and an invigilator will come to you. Do not talk to anyone until you have left the exam room, and listen carefully to any instructions that are given.

When the exam starts, don't panic. Take time to read the questions, and decide which ones you are going to answer if the choice of questions is optional. Pick ones you feel comfortable with and read them again carefully. How you approach the question can make the difference between a good response and a poor one.

APPROACHING THE QUESTIONS

Lecturers are looking for several things in your response to a question:

- An answer that has a logical argument.
- A demonstration of your knowledge of a subject.
- A clear focus on the question.

Superficial information takes up time in the exam, and does not help you get extra marks. What you need is to plan your response so that everything you write is relevant to the question. The first thing is to read the question carefully and consider what is being asked of you.

Example question

Q1: Discuss the similarities between *Lady Snowblood* (1973, Fujita Toshya) and *Kill Bill* (2003, Quentin Tarantino). Support your discussion with detailed analysis of at least two scenes.

The key elements in this question are based around two films (let's assume you have studied them both on your course) so your knowledge of them will have to be displayed in your response – but how? What are the key words in the question above?

Identify key words

Discuss

The term states that you need to create an argument and demonstrate the processes by which you reach your conclusions. Similar words include: debate, argue, explore, comment.

Similarities

When considering similarities it is important to explore a number of different elements. These could include: imagery, themes, narrative, costume, soundtrack, characterisation, cinematography, etc.... Similar words include compare, contrast.

Support

Remember that your arguments need to rest on evidence from films or critical readings. Any claims that you make need to be substantiated. Similar words include: substantiate, provide evidence.

Analysis

It is important not to produce a simple list of observations but to develop a few key areas. All your points should fit within an overall argument. One approach is to choose a scene from each film and produce detailed textual analysis comparing the two to support your overall argument. Similar words include evaluate, examine, study and investigate.

Now we know what the question is asking, the next thing is to plan what you are going to say.

PLANNING YOUR RESPONSE

Your answer has to be clearly structured so you cover all the aspects of the question. Before you start writing your full response, take a couple of minutes to work out a rough plan. Remember, when you have finished, to draw a neat line through your plan to show it is not part of your answer. It all helps to show your expertise and approach to the question.

The key thing is to focus on what you know and feel confident talking about. Introduce your topic briefly, with any key points or facts that you think you can extend in your answer. Pick out the elements of the topic that you feel are linked to the question, and remember to provide evidence. Discuss key texts and theories that are pertinent. At this level of study, it is how you develop and discuss ideas that are important: remember it is not how much you write that is important, but the quality of your work.

TIMING IN THE EXAM

Planning your time in an exam is one of the most important factors. A lot of students worry about running out of time, and watch the clock rather than focus on their answer. Set yourself a target for when each question has to be done, but do not worry if you overrun slightly. If time is running out, summarise main points and arguments to simple, relevant paragraphs, sentences and/or bullet points. Don't give up with a few minutes left; just do your best to set out your ideas. This way, even though your answer may not be as detailed as you would have like you have still attempted to answer the question.

TIME'S UP

One of the most depressing things following an exam is the post-mortem. Discussing your answers with friends is likely to result in you questioning your approach and analysis. Don't focus on any one weakness or a small detail that you may have got wrong or omitted to include. Relax and enjoy the fact that it is over.

Chapter 17

Presentation skills

Dave Allen

PREPARATION FOR DISCUSSION

Think about the following questions:

- How do you feel about giving presentations in front of other students?
- Why are presentations important?
- Do you have any fears?
- Are you looking forward to giving presentations?
- Are they a fair form of assessment?

INTRODUCTION

Presentations are increasingly used as forms of assessment at university. This adds variety to the methods of assessment but it is also tied to universities' increasing desire to offer experiences that will help students in later life. They are intended to help you to develop confidence in addressing other people as this is a key element of tasks in future work and social life. Although the experience can be challenging, this is a skill that more and more employers are demanding. Presentations will also prepare you for the interview process which you will no doubt encounter on leaving university.

PRESENTATION STYLES AND APPROACHES

There are quite a number of films and television programmes that feature live presentations as key elements of the narrative – particularly presentations in professional working environments and/or courtrooms. Consider the following three examples and associated questions which may be useful to study (although you may be able to identify alternative films to these three and apply the same questions):

1. *Disclosure* (Barry Levinson, 1994) starring Demi Moore (Meredith Johnson) and Michael Douglas is a film about institutional power and sexuality. There are key moments when Johnson makes a technically impressive PowerPoint presentation. The mise-en-scène is full of very specific lighting, technology and costumes which clearly establish Moore's *apparent* power (see Figure 17.1).

Figure 17.1 Disclosure (Barry Levinson, 1994).

- Is it a good presentation?
- Which aspects of it work?
- How does it compare with presentations in educational institutions?
- Can you learn any lessons from it?

2. Atticus Finch (Gregory Peck) in *To Kill a Mockingbird* (Robert Mulligan, 1962) (Figures 17.2 and 17.3) makes a courtroom presentation in a very different style from Moore in *Disclosure*.

Figure 17.2 To Kill a Mockingbird (Robert Mulligan, 1962).

167

Figure 17.3 To Kill a Mockingbird (Robert Mulligan, 1962).

- How is his presentation different from Demi Moore's?
- Who is he addressing? Is it everyone in that room?
- What are the features that make him so impressive?

3. By contrast, there is an episode of BBC TV's *The Office* (series 2, episode 4) in which David Brent (Ricky Gervais) appears with a reversed baseball cap and jeans and offers a typically embarrassing improvised presentation to a group of bewildered employees in an austere office space (Figure 17.4). By contrast to Demi Moore, Gervais dresses down.

- Why does he do this? Might this ever work?
- Could improvisation ever work?
- It is clearly a model for what *not* to do, but how and why?

COMMUNICATING YOUR IDEAS

There are many ways of communicating your ideas in presentations, all of which should be used to make your ideas clear and

Figure 17.4 The Office (Series 2, Episode 4).

interesting. Remember that while PowerPoint and film clips will certainly help in this aim, content is still the most important element in any presentation. Your ideas need to be well-researched, and you need to demonstrate that you have read widely and know what you are talking about.

Visual aids and other materials

PowerPoint: this is one of the most commonly used means of disseminating information in lectures and presentations. However, it is not always wisely used. Be careful not to include too much information and too much text. Make sure the font is large enough to be easily read. Is the text legible? Choose your colours carefully (e.g. avoid pink writing on a red background). Select your images carefully and think about where to position them (make sure images do not obscure the text). Don't simply read from your slides without adding additional information; PowerPoint should provide key points which you develop.

OHPs/visualiser: before there was PowerPoint many students and lecturers used an overhead projector (OHP) to display information. This would involve writing on transparent sheets of plastic in a permanent marker. Many teaching rooms at universities still have the facility to show OHP slides. If this is your chosen mode of address then make sure your handwriting is clear (legible and large enough). If you are not confident that you have neat handwriting then you may want to consider photocopying a word-processed document onto a transparency. The visualiser is an updated version of the OHP. The visualiser will project an image of anything (a typed document, a page from a book, a photograph, a work of art etc.) that you place on the machine.

Cue cards: although these may seem like an old-fashioned tool, many students find these useful in delivering presentations to a class. They allow information to be communicated without simply reading from a script and act as a reminder of the key points.

Film clips: presentations are greatly enriched by the use of relevant film clips to illustrate your points. However, these need to be used carefully. Make sure that you are familiar with the equipment in the room in which you are talking. Can you play both DVD and video? It is a good idea to make a DVD or video of clips. If you are unable to do this, either set your video at the correct place or ensure you know which chapter and the exact time of the specific film clips. Make sure they are not too long or short and that they are there for a reason. Also, comment on them and engage in appropriate textual analysis. Remember, too many clips can eat into your presentation time, and it is also a good idea to set up your clips before you start talking.

Still images: you don't need to illustrate all your points with film clips; still images can be a useful way of highlighting your ideas and can be easily embedded into a PowerPoint presentation. This is a way of engaging in textual analysis and is ideal when you only have a short time. It also alleviates any worries about technology. Still images can be found in many places, including books, magazines and the internet. Alternatively, you can capture images from films using DVD software packages on your computer.

Handouts: providing students with handouts is a good way of engaging your audience and demonstrating that you are well prepared. Think carefully about what you should include. Do not give unnecessary information, such as the entire written text. Good examples of handouts include quotations, further readings, bibliography and images.

WORKING IN A GROUP

You may be required to deliver group presentations, for which you need to consider the following areas: working with other people, planning and organisation, allocating tasks and identifying appropriate roles. The French existential philosopher Jean-Paul Sartre once defined Hell as 'other people'. If you are required to make an assessed presentation to your class you may well discover what he meant. A key part of the challenge of a group presentation is that you need to be organised collectively – both practically (right place, right time) and academically (right material, right medium). You also need to ask the lecturer whether it is a requirement that every group member speaks and presents material. If it is not, how do you decide who will do what? Here is a list of pros and cons for you to consider when embarking on a group presentation.

Pros

- You will share responsibility for the presentation.
- The anxiety you feel may be reduced.
- You will learn to work in a group.
- Roles can be allocated according to group members' strengths and interests.
- It is more fun working together.

- You will develop organisational skills (i.e. maintaining contact with group members).
- You will become more aware and respectful of other people's ideas.

Cons

- You may encounter unreliable team members.
- The group mark may not reflect everybody's involvement and effort.
- You cannot work at a time that just suits you.
- You may have to compromise in terms of your ideas and input.

DEALING WITH GROUP ISSUES

You will normally be given reasonable preparation time and if there is a serious issue with one member of the group that you are unable to resolve, then the issue needs to be raised with your tutor in good time. Otherwise, it is your collective responsibility to do the best you can.

It is occasionally the case that individual group members will feel that their (group) mark is significantly lower than their usual individual grades. Tutors may cite poor group dynamics or an unreliable group member as the reason for this. Put simply, that's the reality of group work as it is with team games – it is good preparation for life. It will be your collective responsibility to work together to make the presentation successful.

TIPS AND ADVICE (GROUP OR INDIVIDUAL)

- What have you been asked to prepare? What is the focus and how will you address it?
- Always ensure that you have researched your topic and that this is evident in your talk (use academic books, journals and the internet).

- Organise your ideas; try not to include too much material, information, or too many facts and ideas.
- Is there a time limit on your presentation (the answer is almost certainly yes)? If so, how will you organise your material?
- Be aware of the technology available in room, and make sure that you know how to use it.
- Be prepared for technological failures and have a back-up plan; e.g. print off your PowerPoint slides; see if there is an appropriate clip on youtube.com in case of problems with the DVD.
- Although content is important, think about the way you present yourself. Try to find the balance between entertaining and informing the audience.
- Speak clearly and not too fast.
- Wherever possible, do not read your notes verbatim. Try using bullet points as an aid.
- Think about your body language; are you more comfortable standing or sitting? Ensure you do not turn your back on the audience or obscure any visual aids.
- Try to make eye contact with everyone in the room, not just the tutor.

THE AUDIENCE

How can you make use of the presence of audience members? Will they need some written information, and if so when, why and for what purpose? Will the written material raise questions, offer information or will it provide follow-up materials. When is the best point to distribute it?

What about questions? On many occasions, student presentations finish with a slide or spoken 'any questions?' followed by silence in the class, a palpable sense of relief among the presenters and a quick 'thank you', followed by a scurry for the seats. Is there a better way of doing things? Should questions always be the last thing? Do they have to be left to individuals or could they be asked by groups, following a brief discussion?

What about your appearance? Is what you wear important? Make sure that you feel confident in what you have chosen to wear, and that it is appropriate for the occasion. What really matters is that your audience is convinced that you are interested in, even excited by, the topic and the ideas. In some ways your enthusiasm may be the single most important factor in engaging that audience.

Finally, what is your role as a member of the audience? There is nothing worse when you are doing presentations than to be met with bored, vacant expressions. Try to be encouraging to the speaker; nods and smiles can really help with confidence. It is also important to ask questions when prompted and to contribute to any discussions.

SEMINAR EXERCISE

Prepare to deliver a 15-minute group presentation, based on one of the following questions:

1   Provide an analysis of a film of your choice considering production history, visual style and its importance in cinema history.
2   Present an introduction to an important director, concentrating on his/her film-making characteristics and his/her place in film history.
3   Consider the importance and historical relevance of an important film studio.

Critical reading is required for the presentations.

FINAL CHECK LIST

Planning	If you are preparing a group presentation you need to plan who will say what, and how each section will link together.
Delivery	How do you plan to deliver your information? Will you stick to a script, use aide-memoires or improvise?
Technology	Will you use PowerPoint, or a visualiser? What about other forms of multimedia? Video, DVD?
Audience	Ensure that you pitch your information at the appropriate level for your audience. Try and make your presentation as interesting as possible.
Content	Make sure you have researched your topic extensively. Be careful not to include too much information. Maintain focus throughout and be aware of time constraints.
Assessment	Be aware of the marking criteria; do you know what the assessor is looking for?

Chapter 18

Screenwriting

Craig Batty

As part of your Film Studies course, it is likely that you will at some point encounter screenwriting. This may be in the form of critical study, analysing the work of a particular screenwriter for example, but hopefully you will have the chance to explore screenwriting from a practical perspective. Screenwriting as a form does exactly what it says – writes for the screen. Although this may seem obvious, there is an inherent principle within this – visuality – that you need to keep reminding yourself of. Many student screenplays begin by sounding much more like radio or theatre plays, heavy with dialogue and little attention paid to the use of vision to tell the story. As Charlie Moritz points out, '[p]arallels have often been drawn between watching screen dramas . . . and the experience of dreaming . . . wherever possible, the pictures and the action should always come first. It is what we are watching which truly engages our interest' (2001, 47). As part of the film-making process, screenwriters have to understand that audiences *see* as well as *hear*; it is therefore vital to incorporate this effectively into practice.

Although screenwriting shares common traits with other forms of creative writing, such as the use of plot, character and voice (found in novels, short stories, poetry etc.), it is a very *particular* art form. Here are some specific ideas about the nature of screenwriting:

- A screenplay is a blueprint for the next stage of production. Unlike a novel, the screenplay is only the end-product of the pre-production process of film-making. It literally comes to life during casting, rehearsal, production, editing and distribution.

- Screenwriting is often seen as more technical and formulaic than other forms of creative writing. It can be perceived as mechanical as opposed to organic and creative, though this is perhaps a misunderstood idea.

- It is heavily reliant upon planning. Screenplays often sell solely on their treatment (prose version of the story) or step-outline (scene-by-scene synopsis), not necessarily after the script has been written.

- It can be seen as a business-oriented practice. Many screenplays are written for a particular genre, packaged and shaped according to how the market operates.

- Screenwriting is a collaborative process. It is constantly reworked following feedback from development producers, script editors and directors.

Nevertheless, the art of screenwriting should not be underestimated. Screen stories can take shape from very personal experiences and can be written with a unique writer's voice. How original they are will depend upon the writers themselves, such as how established and 'trusted' they are, but also upon the context in which the screenplay is operating: Hollywood studios, independent outfit, mainstream TV broadcaster, first-time independent producer/director, etc.

Having established the nature and context of screenwriting, the rest of this chapter will explore four key areas of the writing process which will give you a basic but firm understanding of how screenplays are formed. (It should be noted here that these discussions relate primarily to mainstream cinema.) The areas of exploration are:

- Story and structure
- Character

- Genre
- Building scenes

STORY AND STRUCTURE

A very useful place to start with understanding screen story structure is the classical **three-act structure**. This method, literally incorporating beginning, middle and end, is a way of ordering information into a plot to effectively tell a story that the audience will understand (and hopefully connect to.) Using Syd Field's model (2003, 9–18) as a basis, the three acts are as follows:

Act One, Setup (¼) – This introduces the central characters (namely the protagonist) of the film and the story world in which it is set, and establishes the underlying theme or premise driving the narrative. Through the inciting incident (see below) the goal or desire of the protagonist is identified; this is what they will have to achieve by the end of the film. The setup should make clear what the protagonist has at stake, i.e. what he or she stands to lose if the goal is not achieved. It should also pinpoint the antagonists of the film, hinting at the problems and hurdles that the protagonist will have to overcome in order to successfully achieve the goal.

Act Two, Confrontation (½) – This is where the action of the film truly starts. Having decided to undertake the challenge to achieve the goal, the protagonist's journey begins and progresses at speed. Obstacles and hurdles are met and overcome along the journey, testing the protagonist and their determination to accomplish this challenge. Conflict is key. New situations are experienced, developing the protagonist's knowledge and awareness of others, and friends and enemies are made. Central to the confrontation is that the protagonist begins to learn inner lessons; their character emotionally 'grows'.

Act Three, Resolution (¼) – The film begins to wind-down or change direction when the protagonist gets or does not get what they want (challenge.) The goal is usually achieved, but sometimes it is achieved in a different way than expected, or not achieved at all. The protagonist, usually with the 'treasure' of the challenge in hand, goes back to their normal world. This time, however, they have gained new knowledge and insights into themselves and the world. They have changed, and often have rid themselves of the problem they had at the start. They have learned lessons and ask themselves, how will life be different from now on?

The core of a screenplay, binding these three acts together, is the **character journey** (see, for example, Campbell (1993) and Vogler (1999)). All mainstream films are about the journey of one or more characters from one place to another. This may be an obviously physical journey, such as a road movie, or a more emotional journey such as a coming-of-age story. Most films combine the two.

The **physical journey** concerns itself with what the protagonist literally *wants*. The audience sees them trying to physically achieve an external goal. This might include:

- Getting to a place (by a certain time) – *Road Trip*, *Thelma and Louise*, *Big Fish*, *Transamerica*, *Little Miss Sunshine*.
- Finding a way home/out of a situation – *The Wizard of Oz*, *Finding Nemo*, *Cold Mountain*, *Chicago*, *The Magdalene Sisters*.
- Getting someone's attraction /attention – *Four Weddings and a Funeral*, *Notting Hill*, *Date Movie*, *Along Came Polly*, *The Science of Sleep*.
- Rescuing the victim – *Ransom*, *Hostage*.
- Finding the killer/criminal – *Scream*, *I Know What You Did Last Summer*, *Halloween*, *The Texas Chainsaw Massacre*, *The Interpreter*.

The **emotional journey** works in parallel but asks: what does the protagonist really *need*? The audience sees them develop emotionally as a result of undertaking the physical journey. These ideas might include:

- Realising who they really are – *discovering new knowledge about themselves.*
- Learning to love – *disposing of guilt and grief in order to let someone into their lives once again.*
- Finding inner happiness – *having battled through the external world, being content with who they are inside or realising that they are valued after all.*
- Sparking the imagination – *gaining a new lease of life and momentum to go on and start something new or approach with fresh eyes.*

Notice here the differentiation between what a character *wants* and what a character *needs*. Often it is the want that is obvious to the protagonist and the audience initially, but then it develops into an understanding of the need. By the end, it is not uncommon for the need to have taken precedence; the story is about the emotion over the action.

To pull the above ideas of structure and journeys together, here is a common narrative shape of mainstream film:

The **disturbance** in a character's life sets them on a **journey** to achieve their **want** (and **need**), where **obstacles** stand in their way, creating **dramatic conflict** for the character to **overcome** before **resolution** can be found.

In his highly acclaimed book *Story* (1999), Robert McKee poses six key questions which can be used by writers to test the skeleton frame of their story. These are also useful for screenwriting students learning to unpick a narrative. The questions are:

181

- Who are the characters?
- What do they want?
- Why do they want it?
- How do they go about getting it?
- What stops them?
- What are the consequences? (1999, 19)

> **SEMINAR EXERCISE**
>
> Using these questions as a basis, can you identify the narrative frame of a mainstream film? Can you say what happens in each of the three acts? Can you identify a combination of physical and emotional journeys?

Motivation within a narrative is crucial. If the protagonist has no impetus to start the journey, other than 'ok, I may as well,' then the story lacks conviction and will probably end up being rather banal. What often drives the narrative is a deep desire; an emotional attachment to the goal which will develop and, by the end of the second act, may feel like a matter of life and death. For this motivation to be set in action, within Act One there needs to be an **inciting incident**. This is the disturbance to the protagonist's normal world – a 'call to adventure' (Vogler, 1999, 99–106) – which propels them into the journey. It comes in the form of a problem or challenge which sets the story in motion. It is the true beginning of the story because it is the moment where the stakes are set and the protagonist has to understand the call and act upon it. Without the inciting incident there would be no story because there would be no moment of crisis where the protagonist has to make a decision to undertake a challenge and begin a journey. The inciting incident comes in any form, but may include the following:

- Someone sets a challenge – *the task is to complete the challenge by the deadline given.*

- Boy meets girl for the first time – *he realises he must chase her and they will fall in love* (gay narratives subvert this traditional boy/girl pattern).

- Someone sees something they want – *they start a journey to try and get it by whatever means*.

- Someone dies or is fatally injured – *this could be the moment where someone is forced to start a new life without this person; or it could be that the death triggers a plot of revenge and affirmation*.

The final key structural element to understand in screenwriting is the notion of the **act turning point**; literally, the points at which the action changes and moves one act into the next. Syd Field calls these **plot points**: 'any incident, episode, or event that "hooks" into the action and spins it around into another direction' (2003, 14). So, a plot point or act turning point is a pivotal moment of action which takes Act One into Act Two, and Act Two into Act Three.

The first plot point, usually occurring at a quarter of the film in, can be understood as any moment which represents *the decision to act*. Here, the protagonist has understood what is at stake from the inciting incident and feels impelled to move forward. Quite simply, the character's journey physically begins. It needs to be a big moment of the narrative because, having taken the decision to go on and undertake the challenge, there is no going back. Here are some manifestations of plot point one:

- A journey physically begins – *the bags are packed and they leave the house; the aeroplane doors lock and it takes to the skies; the first steps are taken on the Yellow Brick Road*.

- Someone starts out for revenge – *the first attempt is made to seek the killer; the first point of the revenge plot is planned; they leave the building and begin to hunt down the culprit*.

- Something is sought/hunted – *the protagonist begins to compile the relevant information; an old contact who 'knows everything' is*

> *called to arrange a meeting; the vehicle is purchased to help with the chase.*

■ The challenge is undertaken – *the first task begins; they re-read the instructions so that they get it right; Lester gets out his weights and begins to get fit for Angela.*

■ The chase for boy/girl starts – *the first date is sought; she calls her friends to find out all she can about him; he buys roses ready to present to her that night.*

Some act turning points may not be so obvious on a first viewing but, once the story has been seen/read from beginning to end, it is quite easy to go back and see where the act breaks occurred. Of course there are no scientific ways of measuring them, and many screenwriting books offer alternative analyses of such structural elements, but the list above gives you a pretty clear insight into how the first-act turning point can take shape. The second-act turning point, taking the confrontation into the resolution, usually occurs when what has been the goal of the narrative is (or is not) achieved. It is often a dark moment where all seems lost and unobtainable, but, with the strength and will of the protagonist, the treasure is taken in hand. Sometimes new pieces of information or new revelations provide the clue or the impetus for the protagonist to finally win. They may be about to give up, but the big moment of the turning point spurs them on to succeed. The film does not end there of course; there is the resolving of the story to do, and sometimes films make their characters go through one more final challenge before they can go back home. But more often than not the second plot point is a climactic moment where all seems lost and dead, but then the protagonist vows to keep on and win. Examples include:

■ A journey finally ends after a breathless race, the hero taking the prize.

■ Someone or something is found, moments before it is too late.

- The murderer is revealed, just in time before a second deadly act is committed.
- After provocation and a seemingly lost cause, someone admits defeat.
- After a huge mix-up, the couple eventually fall in love; or at least agree to date.

From this moment in the narrative, something has changed about the story. Often, the internal, emotional need of the protagonist has taken over the drive of the story and they begin to learn the true value of the journey undertaken. The physical journey may be cast aside, and the true substance of the story (theme) lived and celebrated.

BREAKING THE RULES

Although the mainstream form of storytelling is the most prominent in our culture, some film-makers choose to break the rules. Or so they think. In fact, as a Film Studies student you perhaps inhabit the privileged position of being one of those who wants to defy the set patterns! There are two key things to say here.

1 Of course you can break the rules. Rules are there to be broken. However, you must still consider your audience. If you change the shape of a story, or rip it to shreds totally, will the audience still want to watch? If nothing happens, and the characters do not actively pursue a goal, then there is a chance that audiences will turn off.

2 Even if you think you are breaking the rules, perhaps making a point about defying 'the system', the chances are that you are not *really* breaking the rules. You may be using them in a different way, or being more subtle about the narrative framework, but it is likely that the core of your screenplay is still informed in some way by an understanding of classical structure.

185

Either way, a useful book you may wish to consult is Linda Aronson's *Screenwriting Updated* (2001). Her book looks at various forms of 'new' storytelling, such as parallel stories and sequential narratives, but the premise of the book is that these are ways of *adapting* and *re-working* traditional structures.

> **SEMINAR EXERCISE**
>
> Choose a film which you think defies the rules of mainstream storytelling. Write why you think this is so. Now go back to the film and see if you can identify elements which originate from mainstream storytelling. Can the rules be re-applied? Is the narrative structure really that different? Some useful examples might include: *Donnie Darko, Requiem for a Dream, Brick, Mysterious Skin, Hidden, Lost in Translation.*

CHARACTER

One of the first things to understand about character is that it is a concept which is tightly linked to story and structure. Robert McKee postulates, 'structure *is* character. Character *is* structure' (1999, 100). What this means is that the plot is driven by the character; the story does not happen unless it is pulled along by a strong sense of character motivation. This is apparent in the details of story and structure above, but to summarise:

- The story only really happens so that the audience can chart a character's growth or inner development.
- The story is brought about by the inciting incident, which is often tied to the character's dramatic problem or inner turmoil (see physical and emotional).
- The plot, in other words the physical journey undertaken, is mapped out and shaped by the emotion of the character.

Choices they make and decisions played out form the path of the journey, not necessarily the other way around.

Character as screen persona (characterisation) is most commonly understood as the physical presence on screen. This is true because the heart of the story and the crux of the emotional journey can only be brought about by the actions of characters. For this reason it is useful to think about characters as *tools* of story, used in ways to live out the plot, connect audiences to the narrative and persuade them of the story that is being told. There are a range of characters in operation in a screenplay, the **protagonist**, **main characters**, **secondary characters** and **minor characters**, but here we will just look at the protagonist, or 'hero' of the story. There may of course be more than one, seen for example in multiple protagonist and parallel narratives: *About A Boy*, *Before You Go*, *Magnolia*, *Sliding Doors*, *The Hours*, *The Banger Sisters*. Here are some common features of the protagonist:

- This is *their* story. We watch them, root for them and often project ourselves onto them.
- They should be likeable in order for the audience to connect with them.
- They are active agents in the story, driving the story forward and making decisions which affect the shape of the narrative. They are not passive.
- They occupy the majority of the screen time, and sometimes take on the role of narrator.
- The story is seen from their point of view with their agenda framed.
- The key to a protagonist is that he or she changes throughout the course of a screenplay. They develop emotionally and sometimes physically.

Developing characters is an integral part of the writing process. Not only do they have to have the dramatic drive and emotional integrity as outlined, but they have to be well rounded, credible and appealing to watch. Although at heart many protagonists are similar, such as someone who needs to overcome grief before they can trust again, the way that characters are presented is somewhat unique. Each screenwriter will unearth a different back-story (where the character has come from), portray different physical attributes and have a strong sense of social attitude and outlook which will make their creation different to any already seen elsewhere. This is what makes characters likeable, lovable and memorable.

SEMINAR EXERCISE

What is your favourite film? Who is the protagonist? Make a list of some of the reasons why this character is so likeable. What makes them unique? Why do we want to spend time with them?

Once the inner fabric of a character has been developed, the execution for the screen should begin to come together. Remembering that screenwriting is a visual medium, it is useful to approach screen characters from the point of view of what the audience sees. Here are some ideas about how characters can be approached visually.

Action and behaviour

How does your character behave in a given situation? Depending on their attitude and point of view, they are bound to act in a certain way and react to people in a mode that suits their personality. For example, how does he react to people who think they are superior to him? How does he treat those who openly criticise people and put the world to rights? Action and behaviour clearly depict character, telling the audience who the character is, what they feel, how they operate and what subtextually lies beneath anything they do (again, choice determined by inner being.) A good exercise to develop this is by putting your character into a scenario, perhaps one alien to him, and letting him 'naturally' react. This will give you new insights into who they are.

Appearance

What does your character wear? What does your character not wear? How do they present themselves, and is it always in the same way? Working with physical appearance is useful because it can be seen as a visual expression of identity. So, if your character is the kind of person who loves everyone and everything and welcomes any situation, visually depicting this by the look of the character is a quick and effective way of informing the audience of this. Images are instant and the audience will decode the signs more easily than you may think. Other than bodily appearance techniques (clothes, accessories, body art, posture, presence), the appearance of the environment of a character can also be used to inscribe character. For example, what is their home like? What does it say about their personality? What kind of lifestyle do they have? This can include car, social scene, holiday destination, hobbies and interests, and fashion.

Job

What job does your character do? Is she a hairdresser? Is she a legal executive? Often screenplays open with the character doing their job, which is a quick and effective visual method to say so much about the character: level of hierarchy, responsibility, qualifications, income, how they are viewed by others etc. Even though the job is happening here and now, it actually tells an audience so much about where the character has come from. Within a job, the character may also have another role, one which they have perhaps chosen themselves. In any organisation there are people who do first aid, organise social events, represent the union, coordinate

189

certain aspects of the business and so forth. These are ways in which a character has *appropriated* their job to suit their individual needs and skills. Again, this is highly illustrative of personality and can be used effectively.

Voice and language

If appearance is a visual expression of identity, then the voice and language of a character is a vocal expression of identity. Sometimes characters have very particular ways of speaking which suit their personality, such as if they mumble or stumble through sentences. The vocabulary they use can also be highly evocative of attitude and presence. If a character uses highly convoluted sentences and high-brow vocabulary, then it is likely that they are trying to convey a sense of authority and superiority. This may in turn mean that underneath they feel worthless or a failure. However your character is at heart, their dialogue can be used to express this.

As detailed, the development and execution of character is twofold. Firstly it has to be linked intrinsically to the nature of story; the inner emotion and fabric of a character which takes them on their journey. Secondly, the character's inner being is manifest on the screen in various ways, from appearance and job to behaviour and voice. All the writing should be geared towards telling an audience what a character is like and how they are feeling/reacting emotionally to the journey. Here are some quick exercises to help with creating and developing characters:

- **Back-story** – write a history of your character. Where have they come from? What have they experienced in their life? How have they got to be in the position they are now? The key outcome of this task is to discover the reasons why your character behaves the way they do, which will then be used to develop the story further. Pick out the key turning points in their life which have added to the motivations for their current state.

- **Monologue** – write a piece from the point of view of the character. You could start by giving them a question (who do you hate most? why are you not working today?) or put them in a situation (trapped in a lift, sitting on a beach.) The writing should be organic and continuous, not forced. This way you will get a natural feel for your character's voice and for how they think about things. Read this back and note any major revelations/discoveries.

- **Visual portrait** – collect images which represent your character. These may be pieces from magazines or newspapers, or symbols which you think mean something. The images as a portrait should tell you about personality, lifestyle, attitudes and environment (work, home, social.) Use these to remind yourself of the character's being as you write the screenplay, so that you do not stray away from staying true to them. Some of the images may even be used in the screenplay, such as places and objects.

- **Visual story** – choose one or two adjectives that describe your character and show them using a visual sequence only. Put the character into a situation and let the adjectives dictate the action. This is useful for reinforcing how when writing the screenplay you will display the character's personality primarily by visuals. In this case, actions speak louder than words.

GENRE

McKee rightly notes that 'the audience is already a genre expert. It enters each film armed with a complex set of anticipations learned through a lifetime of moviegoing' (1999, 80). More than ever, film (and increasingly television) is produced and packaged according to a raft of genres which the audience understands, affiliates itself to and somewhat craves. For a screenwriter this is a vital element of development, not just because the screenplay needs to be sold but because the genre of a project has different demands on the writing. Most people will understand genre as to mean a particular type, with specific codes and conventions that an audience comes to be familiar with. As Glen Creeber points out, genre is 'the product of a text- and audience-based negotiation activated by the viewer's expectation' (2001, 7). The key here is that genre is not only an audience-focused concept but one which has to work within the text itself; in other words, the screenplay has to correctly embody the genre. The concept of genre is a huge one, and many books have been written on it. For this chapter, it is useful to look at a few ways in which genre can affect how a screenplay is written.

Story and structure

The genre in question has an intrinsic influence on the story type and how it is told. As already detailed, all screenplays are about journeys and characters' development. This is the basic concept. Employing genre will still have this journey at heart, but will shape it in a distinct direction. For example, a **romantic comedy** is always about the chase between two lovers. The inciting incident is relative to this – they meet – and the whole narrative is driven by the conflict of the two pushing and pulling each other and, for the majority, not getting on. The story develops until they do eventually get on, and the climax of the film comes in the form of a well-awaited reunion. There are variations to this of course, but this is the basic generic demand of the romantic comedy. **Horror/ slasher** films have demands too. The inciting incident here, usually occurring early on as a hook, is a death of some gruesome sort. The narrative then drives towards finding out who the killer is, all the while other victims falling foul to the maniac. The climax of the film comes in the revelation of the killer, often with some kind of explanation as to why they committed the crime. In a **sports** film, the story is almost always one of a protagonist who needs to prove him or herself, using the means of playing sport as an extension of the inner anguish which needs to be healed. Being part of a team is crucial to this narrative, making friends and enemies and using them to prove worth, and the climax of the film requires some kind of big, special match in which the protagonist will get the chance to show to the world who they are and what they are capable of.

Character

Genre places similar demands on character, namely the protagonist. In a **detective** film the audience will expect a renegade cop, out to set the world to rights but at the same time perhaps solve their own inner struggle. The detective will usually also have a side-kick, who although less experienced will bring something special to the quest and to helping the detective's own personal journey. In a **Western**, the lone hero is the driving force of the story. He is a wandering nomad who goes from town to town, often a chip on his shoulders and venting his anger on the bad and evil. **Science fiction** films will employ a similar lone hero type of character, this time their battle with 'aliens' representing the fear of the future and confronting a changing, technological world. The hero will be wounded internally too, using the battles and confrontations as an excuse to avoid the inner turmoil. Like the Western, these films will usually climax with a one-to-one showdown with the major antagonist, and for character this represents a showdown with the self and cleansing of the emotional wound.

Visual grammar

The visual grammar of a film varies wildly according to its genre. In other words, how the film looks and feels gives instant clues to its type. This can be a combination of story, design and direction, coming together to stay true to audience expectations. Visual grammar, mise-en-scène, includes:

- *Colour* – is it a dark, eerie thriller? A light, bright comedy? Colour used in set design, costume and filmic tone can evoke a strong sense of genre.
- *Objects* – knives, scissors and boiling pans in a slasher? Flying horses and hidden chests of elixir in a fantasy? Objects carry symbolic meaning of the genre; a currency which the audience understands.
- *Costume* – this can represent a genre by adhering to visual expectations. Linked to colour, this can include evocation of period, class, status, mood, environment etc. The clothes tell a story in themselves.
- *Tones* – mainly undertaken by the director, but a writer can understand how setting and lighting can affect tone and mood. The scene may be filmed with a certain hue, or with specific lighting for dramatic effect.

There is much more to understand about genre which this chapter cannot accomplish. For example, many films are hybrids where two or more genres are spliced together. Sometimes too it is hard to tell what genre a film is, especially if it is something not so obvious like a social drama (as compared to, say, a Western.) A useful book for further insight into genre is Ken Dancyger and Jeff Rush's *Alternative Scriptwriting: Successfully Breaking the Rules, 3rd edition* (2002), particularly Chapter 6, 'Working with Genre' and Chapter 8, 'Working Against Genre'.

BUILDING SCENES

The definition of a scene is a moment of action which is contained within one location or one time frame. Its function is to drive the story forward, using characters, setting, action, dialogue and visual grammar. For a scene to work, or for a scene to be vital to the whole narrative, it should contain at least one beat of action. This means that it should have a fragment of story that drives towards the next stage of the plot. This can be simple, such as *A tells B that they must leave*, or it can be more complex, such as *X gives Y an ultimatum, leaving Y feeling that she has nowhere to turn*. This beat of story can be understood as the **transaction** of the scene. Quite literally, this means the 'business' or 'contract' of the scene: what is it there to do? What is its function? When working with the writing of a scene, it is imperative to know what the transaction is. Otherwise, the scene will have no direction and will be very difficult to write. The transaction is the heart of the scene, around which the body can be developed. Charlie Moritz writes: 'If you cut to the heart of what the scene you're dreaming up is about, reduce this to a one-liner, note this down and then build the rest of the scene up around it, you won't miss the scene's meaning or leave it unfocussed' (2001, 98). This is a very useful piece of advice, and in fact in the development process of a screenplay, this is often worked out early on. Some screenwriters produce a step-outline, which in basic terms is a scene-by-scene running summary of the screenplay. Integral to this document is a clear understanding of the function of each scene, and how one by one they piece together to form the full narrative.

SEMINAR EXERCISE

View the opening five minutes of a film. Make a note of all the scenes that take place (i.e. each time the action changes location or time frame) and write, in a line or two, the function of these scenes. Now put these functions together and write a brief summary of the function of the whole of the opening five minutes. What is being set up for the audience? What vital information is provided for this hook into the film?

Finally, scene action. As well as the dialogue, scenes contain screen action / screen direction. Like a theatre's stage directions, these are literally directions for what is happening on the screen at the same time as what is being spoken. They are important for the reader to visualise the action, and as highlighted can provide key moments where the visuals tell the story. This may be on a surface, 'obvious' level, but often visual storytelling can be deeper and more symbolic. Here is how screen directions should be written:

- In the present tense, as if the action is unfolding there and then.
- You should only write what the audience can see. There is no point in detailing character emotion, and worse back-story, because this should be obvious from the action and dialogue.
- They should be tight, fluid and snappy. Overly long, detailed screen directions can slow down the reading process and digress into the realms of prose fiction.
- Long screen directions should be split into smaller paragraphs. A general rule of thumb is that every time the emphasis of the direction changes, as if the camera would focus on something different, a new line should start.

RECOMMENDED READINGS

The following key texts will build upon the basics outlined here, and offer deeper insights and case studies into the areas discussed. They are all widely available and easily accessible.

Aronson, L. *Screenwriting Updated: New (and Conventional) Ways of Writing for the Screen.* California: Silman-James, 2001.

Batty, C. and Waldeback, Z. *Writing for the Screen: Creative and Critical Approaches.* Basingstoke: Palgrave Macmillan, 2008.

Campbell, J. *The Hero with a Thousand Faces.* London: Fontana, 1993. Originally published in 1949.

Dancyger, K. and Rush, J. *Alternative Scriptwriting: Successfully Breaking the Rules* (3rd edn). Woburn, MA: Focal Press, 2002.

Field, S. *The Definitive Guide to Screenwriting*. London: Ebury Press, 2003.

Gates, T. *Scenario: The Craft of Screenwriting*. London: Wallflower, 2002.

Gulino, P. J. *Screenwriting: A Sequence Approach*. New York: Continuum, 2004.

McKee, R. *Story: Substance, Structure, Style and the Principles of Screenwriting*. Methuen: London, 1999.

Moritz, C. *Scriptwriting for the Screen*. London: Routledge, 2001.

Seger, L. *Making a Good Script Great* (2nd edn). California: Samuel French, 1994.

Vogler, C. *The Writer's Journey: Mythic Structure for Storytellers and Screenwriters*. London: Pan Books, 1999.

RECOMMENDED WEBSITES

www.bbc.co.uk/writersroom – *great tips on formatting and submitting scripts*

www.scriptfactory.co.uk – *UK-based script training organisation*

www.script-o-rama.com – *database for downloading free film and television scripts*

www.scriptwritermagazine.com – *base for ScriptWriter Magazine, a highly useful publication dedicated to the scriptwriting industry*

Chapter 19

Practical film-making

Dylan Pank and Karen Savage

In the past, student film-makers made their projects literally on photographic motion picture film, usually 16mm. Motion picture film is difficult to handle. The camera must be kept meticulously clean lest dust marks the surface of the film, ruining the image. The film is developed and printed in specialist labs, and it can be days, possibly weeks, before you see the results. A 400ft roll of film lasts ten minutes before the camera needs reloading in complete darkness. Film cameras do not record audio, so a separate tape deck takes the sound, which has to be synchronised to the picture at the editing stage. In addition, shooting film is expensive: with the cost of the film stock itself, plus developing, printing or transferring to video; even short projects often cost thousands of pounds.

This means many non-professional film-makers approached film production projects with a degree of anxiety, if not fear. Yet film is still considered worth the expense and effort because, until recently, shooting on video with all but the most expensive equipment meant poor-quality images and sound. Film-makers got over the fear factor by painstakingly planning, checking and following procedures to ensure footage was properly exposed, in sync with sound, and sharply focused. Actors rehearsed well or risked wasting valuable film on fluffed lines or missed cues.

That changed with the arrival of DV (digital video) cameras. Even relatively low-cost DV cameras can record an hour of high-quality images and CD-quality sound on cassettes costing only a few pounds. Those images appear instantly on the camera's viewfinder, and within minutes of recording can be transferred to a desktop computer for editing.

However, this convenience can lead to film-makers being sloppy and careless. Once the footage becomes cheap and easily viewed, there seems to be less pressure on film-makers to take those extra steps: they neglect sound, they don't double-check focus, they set exposure carelessly without regard to the mood or impact of the image. In short, everything becomes, in the old phrase, 'near enough for Jazz'. Worse still, some film-makers delegate responsibility for such elements to the camera's automatic features, abdicating all control over the quality of the image.

WHERE TO GET YOUR IDEAS FROM?

Alfred Hitchcock is reputed to have said 'You need three things for a successful film: a good script, a good script and a good script'. A film, be it fictional or documentary, is often a vehicle for telling a story to an audience. However, be careful in developing stories that are either too ambitious or recycled tired ideas and clichés. Overambitious ideas may mean you struggle with complex logistics and techniques beyond your proficiency. It is better to execute a simple idea very well than do something badly that is on far too large a scale. The book *Developing Story Ideas* (Rabiger, 2000) may help you generate ideas. Here are some tips:

- Try not to rely on worn-out storylines lifted from television and movies: the girl walking home at night followed by a sinister stranger, the card game that turns into a shootout, etc.
- Try to think of stories you have heard and experiences you have had in the past that stick in your memory that could be turned into a simple story or scene. You can embellish them with a surprise twist. Urban myths are another possible source of story ideas, if you do not pick over-used stories.

- Brainstorm ideas, digest them and try to think of simple ways to make them fresh and unusual. Don't simply settle for the first version of your idea; keep trying to improve it. The secret of writing is *rewriting*.

The most important thing to keep in mind when developing your film ideas is the audience. The aim of every film is to be watched. Audiences on the whole want to see something entertaining, informative and thought-provoking. You may be taught many important things in terms of script writing and development, story structure, characterisation, how to set out a script proposal and write a properly formatted screenplay, but identifying your audience is the root of the whole enterprise. Also consider the genre of your story: is it a comedy, a thriller or a horror movie? Genre is a concept you'll become very familiar with when studying other films, but also applies to your productions, which will belong to one genre or another, or may combine genres.

COLLABORATION AND TIME MANAGEMENT

Almost all film and video projects are produced in crews. Big-budget productions have crews that number in the hundreds. Even films that appear to have been made by a 'one man band' usually turn out to have a support crew behind them, and even so are the very rare exception rather than the rule. In the overwhelming majority of film production, working well as part of a team is a critical skill. Two of the biggest problems amongst student crews are time management and effective group work. They are, however, among the skills you'll need most after graduating. Use the list below to help organise your shoot.

1   Plan out how much time you are prepared to spend on a project in advance.

201

2   Break the production down into stages and allocate time throughout the semester to complete each stage.

3   Get all members of the crew to agree on how much time they can commit in a week to completing the project.

4   Be clear, honest and frank about how much you are prepared to do.

5   You will be working with people you may not know well, so communicate with your crewmates often.

6   Meet with your crew regularly, as agreed by all of you, for formal meetings to discuss the film progress.

Meetings should be focused towards goals to achieve each week. Some periods will be much busier than others (such as the period allocated to shooting, for example), so some meetings may be short compared to others.

LINES OF COMMUNICATION

Crew members need to:

■   Make sure to have each others' phone numbers and e-mail addresses.

■   Nominate one person to co-ordinate the group.

■   Organise crew responsibilities upfront.

Don't be too specific about crew roles at the start. You may wish to swap roles for camera, sound editing, directing, so each crew member gets a chance to try the different jobs. However, you will need to decide who is in charge of specific tasks for the group. Roles need to be allocated for such seemingly trivial things as getting hold of DV tapes, arranging certain locations, collecting equipment and finding actors or subjects. However, if you do take on a particular role, be clear what the responsibilities are. *Directing the Documentary* (Rabiger, 1992, pp. 59–69) will introduce you to some of the important crew roles found on a typical production.

SEMINAR ACTIVITY

Research the role of one specific crew member (editor, cameraman, director, actor, etc.). Prepare a short presentation explaining the duties and responsibilities that come with that role.

PLANNING

Most films and TV productions, whether they be dramas, documentaries, music videos or corporate films, are made according to a very specific brief, and shot according to a script. There may be room for improvisation, unplanned events or deviation, but in almost all cases the film-makers start with a clear idea of how the film will turn out. This stage is referred to as pre-production, and the success of a project often depends on the clarity of pre-production work. The tools you need at this stage are paper, pencils and a word-processor. Start working with your story as a script, which is a blueprint for the story and structure of the film.

Script formats vary depending on the form you're shooting in, be it a documentary, a TV studio production or a single-camera drama. Formats also vary between institutions. Check which format is suitable for your production. Most screenwriting 'How To' books include a section on script formatting. The script then lays the basis for the following elements:

Storyboard

A visual representation of your film in drawings gives you an idea of how the film will look and be edited. Storyboards don't need to feature brilliant artwork, but their images should indicate how the shots will look through the camera, and give a clear idea of shot composition, space, and if necessary, camera movement (see illustrations in the following storyboards on page 205). The drawings in the first are not very informative, whereas in the second they show more in terms of the camera angle, background and use of space.

Lined script

Scenes in television programmes and films are rarely shown from just one angle, even if the production is filmed with a single camera. Usually a scene is acted out multiple times and the camera moved to capture the scene from different angles. This procedure is known as *coverage* and lining a script helps you plan this. In a lined script, each camera angle is shown as a line running from the point that the angle starts recording from, to the point in the script where it ends. Each line represents a single camera set-up. Typically a set-up, sometimes called the *master shot*, "covers" as much of the scene as possible as a wide-angle shot, then shorter sections might be filmed in close-up. See the example on pages 206–7.

Floor plans

Floor plans are diagrams of your locations seen from above, illustrating camera positions and the arrangement of props, actors and physical objects (such as furniture). This allows you to plan where the camera will be to get particular angles and shots, and how actors might be arranged before the camera. This arrangement of camera and actors is referred to as "blocking".

Schedule

List the dates when each shot in each scene will be filmed. This is done in order to plan the most efficient use of time and resources. Everybody on the crew should have a copy of the schedule to know what they are doing and when. Plan to do the most important material early.

PICTURE	ACTION	SOUND
Scene# 1 Shot # 1 Set-up # 1 	"X" WALKS ALONG THE STREET: LONG SHOT	TRAFFIC NOISE
<u>Scene# 1 Shot # 2 Set-up # 2</u> 	"X" CONTINUES WALKING CLOSE UP	TRAFFIC...

The drawings give little compositional information.

PICTURE	ACTION	SOUND
Scene#1 Shot #1 Set-up # 2 	"X" WALKS ALONG THE STREET: LONG SHOT	TRAFFIC NOISE
Scene# 1 Shot # 2 Set-up #2 	"X" CONTINUES WALKING CLOSE UP	TRAFFIC...

The drawings are still simple, but give a clear idea of space, angle and direction. Storyboard courtesy of John Caro.

20.   EXT.   HOUSE DRIVEWAY – DAY
              MASTER SHOT: WIDE

    The car approaches a country house.
                        MEDIUM SHOT: WILSON

    It parks, and WILSON gets out, briefcase in hand. He trudges

    up the path to the door and knocks. *CLOSE UP: LUCY (OVER*
                                        WILSON'S SHOULDER)

    LUCY ELSON opens the door.

                        LUCY ELSON

                Oh, hello, there. Do come in. Have

                you come a long way?

21.   INT.   HOUSE HALLWAY – DAY
                    MASTER SHOT: TWO SHOT, LUCY AND WILSON

    LUCY leads WILSON along the corridor.

                                                        LUCY ELSON

                I have to say I hope you aren't too

                disappointed if it doesn't all pan

                out. Wendell can be rather picky

about who he works with. We don't get

to watch many films.

                                              WILSON

Well, Mr Bluke has asked me to show

Mr Elson one of our latest

productions.   *CLOSE UP: VIDEO CASSETTE*

He pulls a video cassette out of the briefcase and passes

it to Lucy.

                                              LUCY ELSON

Well, best you wait here and I'll

take it to him.

Wilson hands over the tape.

22.   INT.   LIVING ROOM - DAY
              POINT OF VIEW SHOT OF THE TRAY

LUCY brings in a tray and puts in on the table. On it is the

tape and a glass of milk.

                                              [CONTINUED]

The idea is that if you were unable to make the film, someone else could pick up your pre-production work and make the film as the plans describe. The script, storyboards, lined script floor plans and schedule must all make sense as one overall master plan.

Documentaries are also planned. While you may not have a script, you would have a list of questions and a plan of what material you would need to gather on the location. Storyboards and floor plans could be just as relevant depending on how you plan to shoot material in a given location.

There is a relationship between theory and practice. You should apply your understanding of film theory to your practical work. For example, the films *Blade Runner* (Scott, 1982) and *Delicatessen* (Jeunet and Caro, 1991) are both science-fiction films set in rather grim, dystopian futures, but each has a very different style. *Blade Runner* is largely filmed with telephoto lenses, which compress perspective, giving the sets a crowded claustrophobic feel. These sorts of lenses are also often used in documentaries, and so this style lends *Blade Runner* a more 'realistic' feel, in spite its fantastical setting. *Delicatessen,* on the other hand, predominately uses wide-angle lenses, which exaggerate perspective and depth. If used for a close up, they can distort facial features (see Figures 19.1 and 19.2).

You should research how particular films were shot, and what decisions the film-makers took to achieve the look of certain scenes and the overall style of the movie. This knowledge can be transferred to your own productions. For example, although *American Cinematographer Magazine* focuses on multi-million-dollar

Figure 19.1 Blade Runner (1982) Telephoto lenses compress perspective.

Figure 19.2 Delicatessen (1991) Wide-angle lenses exaggerate depth.

productions, with resources far beyond any student production, you may find ideas and techniques in magazines such as this that can be applied to even the lowest-budget film.

SHOOTING

Production is the stage most people think of when they imagine making a film, but it is often the shortest part of the process. However, it is likely to be the most intensive period of work, and the one that requires the most organisation and teamwork. As part of your pre-production you have prepared a schedule. Try to work within your schedule, but if you fall behind consider whether there are elements you are spending too much time on. Could you combine or abandon material without compromising the coherence of the final film? The production phase is when you will work in concert with almost all your crew members, when group communications and interpersonal skills become most important.

By the time you get to this stage it's vital that you are proficient with the equipment. You should not take equipment without knowing how to use it correctly. If you miss lectures, seminars or workshops on using camera and sound equipment, it's likely that this lack of knowledge will be painfully obvious in your final production. It also lets your colleagues down; they will be carrying the additional workload and, as already stated, teamwork is imperative for a successful production.

While filming, you may find you deviate from your original plan:

- You may find better ways to shoot a scene.
- You may discover that you don't have enough time to get all the coverage you want.
- You may decide that you can shoot a scene with fewer camera set-ups.

However, if you abandon or compress shots without thought it can affect the final results:

- Scenes may not edit together smoothly.
- Sequences will appear to have odd, jarring gaps.
- A shot may linger for too long on one angle, and not cut to the other shots that help tell your story.

It is important to keep track of your material. One crew member should keep a record of all the shots taken, and someone should be continuity supervisor, making sure that the action, hand positions, body movements, costume and hairstyles in different shots will match. These must be consistent as one shot is edited to another, or audiences will notice these continuity errors, which may distract them from the storyline. This paperwork must be kept in an orderly fashion as it will be referred to later by the editor and other post-production workers.

Just as important is sound. You may not record any sound as you shoot, leaving it to the editing stage to add suitable sound effects, music and background sound. This is referred to as 'shooting MOS' and is very common in film and video production and may be suitable for certain productions or some scenes in your projects.[1] However, if you are recording live 'sync' sound, and for any dialogue-based scenes this is often essential, recording good sound is as crucial as shooting good images. Poorly recorded, unclear sound is as bad as out-of-focus or underexposed images, and can be even more frustrating to audiences. As simple a choice as your location can have a major impact on the success of your project. For example, it is a bad idea to try and record an interview in a busy pub or bar, where your subject's voice will compete with other voices, background music and other environmental sound. This background noise is impossible to satisfactorily remove after the fact, and the interview would probably need to be recorded again or rejected during editing.

Finally, important aspects of film production are safety and legality. Do not try to film anything which puts you in danger of causing injury to yourself or others, or which risks damaging private or public property or might find you falling foul of the law. Ensure that you do not trespass on private property or film people without their knowledge or permission. Be aware that you need permission to film on commercial property, even when it is generally open to the public; this will apply to filming in shops, supermarkets, pubs and recreation centres. Finally, if you absolutely must film each other running around with even remotely convincing-looking toy guns, re-enacting a bank robbery, it's probably a good idea to let the local police know what you're doing first.

---

1 The precise reasons for this abbreviation are lost in the mists of time, but it possibly stands for 'Minus Optical Sound', dating back to the early days of film sound when audio was recorded as an image on photographic film. Urban legends about a frustrated German director making his first talkie in Hollywood, demanding to shoot '*Mit Out Sound*', are, at the time of writing, largely uncorroborated.

EQUIPMENT CHECKLIST

It is absolutely essential that you check all equipment before going out on location. When you collect the equipment:

■ Make certain that batteries are fully charged.
■ Check that cameras, tripods and microphones are in good working order.
■ Make sure you have all necessary cables, tapes and accessories.
■ Be pedantic, make a list beforehand and tick each item off as it is checked.

EDITING

The final stages of film production are probably those that have changed the most radically in recent years. Any modern computer is capable of editing high-quality DV material and outputting back to tape or burning it onto a DVD with close-to-professional results. However, all the software gadgets and computing power you can muster will not make up for a lack of care and attention. Many great and groundbreaking films have been made with the most rudimentary film-making tools, but with an abundance of imagination, care and creativity on the part of the film-makers.

The most important commodity an editor has is good footage. The second most valuable is accurate and informative paperwork, from the pre-production and production stages, detailing what has been shot and how they relate to each other. Should these requirements be met, the editor could put the film together, format allowing, with little more that scissors and glue, as indeed many movies in the days of silent film-making were. In more recent times, the director Robert Rodriguez edited many of his early short films with two household VHS recorders, simply copying shots from one deck to the second. The point here is that the equipment does not make the film. Today almost all film and video editing is done on computer, and though the various software and hardware options vary greatly in capability and price, they all adhere to the same principles.

The editing stage is not merely the tidying-up after shooting has finished. Many films have been radically reconceived in the editing room. (You can read examples in Ralph Rosenblum and Robert Karen's *When the Shooting Stops* (1986).) It is often at the editing stage that your film will pick up a particular rhythm and feel. How you edit is often a matter of choice as much as necessity. This will become apparent in your study of such movements as the Soviet montage of the 1920s, or the French New Wave of the 1960s, or the dominant style of the Classical Hollywood system of invisible editing. Even the modern 'MTV' style of rapid editing has its origins in the work of experimental and avant-garde artists.

Below is a list that refers to both good and bad practice for editing.

- If you haven't shot interesting and imaginative material in the production stage, the editing process is unlikely to improve this.
- While footage can be jazzed up by an excess of garish transitions and video filters, these might not distract an audience from the basic lack of content.
- Over-elaborate effects may have a role in a production, but only when integrated coherently into the narrative flow or aesthetic scheme of the film.
- You must properly schedule time to edit your footage well. If editing is rushed it will show up in poor continuity, a lack of rhythm and flow and will cause you to fall back on lazy and unimaginative 'join the dots' style editing.
- Grant yourself the luxury of being able to walk away from the edit. Let it lie for a few days, and then come back to it afresh. As with all stages of film-making, and indeed with all aspects of academic life, time management is an extremely important aspect of post-production.

213

- Work through multiple drafts of the edit until you get a final cut you are happy with. One of the great advantages of editing on a computer, as opposed to older videotape-based editing, is the ability go back and adjust the beginning, middle or end of your film at any time, without needing to re-edit the rest of the film. For this reason computer-based editing is referred to as *non-linear editing* (often known by the abbreviation NLE).

Sound has often become the poor relation of image by the time the film reaches post-production. Mixing and editing sound is often left to the last minute and treated as a tiresome chore or ignored completely. However, the quality of the sound track of your film can be the difference between a successful production and a terrible one. You will do well to remember the following points:

- You need clear, well recorded dialogue. Clean recordings can be made to sound muddy and distorted in post-production, if that's what you want, but to improve badly recorded sound is often hard, and frequently impossible.
- Good sound is a matter of creating layers, not simply 'wallpapering' a scene with pre-recorded pop music. Music comes with its own connotations. A particular song may have a different association for the viewer than the connections you want them to draw from your combination of image and sound.
- Use the soundscape creatively and imaginatively. Consider the effect of silence or moments of peace in contrast with other periods of dense, loud sound.

SEMINAR ACTIVITY

Listen to the soundtrack of a scene from a film without the visuals. List everything you can hear, and say what you think the sound 'means' to you.

Sound should bring what theorist Michel Chion referred to as 'Added Value' (1990, p. 5), as it produces a new layer of knowledge that enriches the visual track, and makes you experience it in a different way. Listening to films is as important as watching, and any great sound film, in any genre, will use sound to inform and energise the drama that you're watching. It helps create the world that is constructed by the film-makers.

FINALLY

As already stated, the point of making a film is to get it seen by an audience. A film (be it made on film or video), like any art, is a form of communication. That does not mean that your film needs to appeal to the broadest number of people. Your intended audience could be very limited and specific. However, before embarking on your film you must consider who your audience is, as it will have profound ramifications on how you choose to address them via the style and content of your film. You will come across examples of 'rules' that film-makers 'must' follow. You may wish to play the role of the iconoclast and question the validity of these rules. Some questions you may want to ask include:

- Why can't the camera cross the 180 line?
- Why does there need to be smooth continuity between one shot and another?
- Why does dialogue need to be clear and audible?
- Does a story need a beginning, a middle and an end?
- Why can't we abandon all these rules?

The 'rules' of traditional film grammar were established in the early days of silent and sound cinema, and have been challenged throughout film history by film-makers such as Dziga Vertov, Maya Deren, Jean-Luc Godard, Lars von Trier among many others. The answers to these questions often depend on who your audience is,

215

and whether your innovations and diversions will act as an aid or an obstruction to their understanding of your film. One thing you will probably discover is any 'rule' you fancy breaking was probably first broken long, long ago, and many times over since.

In the end, making a good film is not a matter of slavishly obeying 'the rules' or satisfying the accepted patterns. Neither is it a matter of reflexively breaking the rules for the sake of it. It is a matter of understanding the principles of film language and using, bending, subverting or rejecting as necessary to get your ideas across to your audience.

BIBLIOGRAPHY

Chion, M. *Audio Vision*. New York: Columbia University Press, 1990.

Jeunet, J. P. and Caro, M. *Delicatessen* [Motion picture]. France: Momentum Pictures, 1991.

Ragiber, M. *Developing Story Ideas*. Oxford: Focal Press, 2000.

—— *Directing the Documentary* (2nd edn). London: Focal Press, 1992.

Rosenblum, R. and Karen, R. *When the shooting stops – the Cutting Begins: A Film Editor's Story*. Da Capo Press: New York, 1986.

Scott, R. *Blade Runner* [Motion Picture]. United States: Warner Brothers, 1982.

Index

219

223